# TABLE OF CONTENTS

| Section | | Page |
|---|---|---|
| 1 | MY LIFETIME DREAMS & GOALS | 4 |
| 2 | MY 12 MONTH GOALS | 5 |
| 3 | MY SCHEDULE & SUCCESS SHEET | 5 |
| 4 | HOW TO TAKE NOTES | 6 |
| 5 | 12 INGREDIENTS OF THE PERFECT DAY | 8 |
| 6 | 31 FACTS ABOUT WISDOM | 10-11 |
| 7 | 31 WISDOM KEYS OF MIKE MURDOCK | 12 |
| 8 | 31 FACTS ABOUT THE HOLY SPIRIT | 14 |
| 9 | 31 FACTS ABOUT YOUR ASSIGNMENT | 16 |
| 10 | 31 FACTS ABOUT THE LAW OF THE SEED | 18 |
| 11 | 31 THINGS GOD WANTS TO INCREASE IN YOUR LIFE | 20 |
| 12 | 8 LEVELS OF SEED-SOWING; MY PERSONAL TESTIMONY | 22-31 |
| 13 | 31 DAYS TO ACHIEVING YOUR UNCOMMON DREAM | 32 |
| 14 | THE COVENANT OF 58 BLESSINGS | 34 |
| 15 | MY 12 MONTH SEED GOALS | 35 |
| 16 | THE WISDOM KEY 3000 | 36 |
| 17 | ONE YEAR BIBLE READING SCHEDULE | 38-39 |
| 18 | READING THE BIBLE THROUGH IN ONE MONTH | 39 |
| 19 | THE LEGACY PROGRAM | 40-43 |
| 20 | THE PRAYER CENTER | 46-48 |
| 21 | THE WISDOM BIBLE PARTNERSHIP EDITION | 50-51 |
| 22 | WISDOM TIMES | 52-54 |
| 23 | MISSION OUTREACHES...HOME OF HOPE...AFRICA...ASIA...MEXICO | 56-65 |
| 24 | UNCOMMON WISDOM GIFT OFFERS | 67-79 |
| 25 | THE MILLIONAIRE 300 | 78-79 |

Unless otherwise indicated, all Scripture quotations are taken from the King James Version of the Bible.
*The Wisdom Center Presents...The School Of Wisdom  ISBN 156394-329-8 (B-238)*
Copyright © 2006 by **MIKE MURDOCK**
All publishing rights belong exclusively to Wisdom International
Editor/Publisher: Deborah Murdock Johnson
Published by The Wisdom Center · 4051 Denton Hwy. · Ft. Worth, Texas 76117· 1-888-WISDOM-1 · (1-817-759-0300)
**Website: TheWisdomCenter.tv**

0906

# ∞ 1 ∞
# MY LIFETIME DREAMS & GOALS

When Your Heart Decides The Destination,
Your Mind Will Design The Map To Reach It.

*-MIKE MURDOCK*

| DATE | GOALS |
|------|-------|
| 1. March 1, 2008 | Become A stay @ home mom |
| 2. | Take |
| 3. | |
| 4. | |
| 5. | |
| 6. | |
| 7. | |
| 8. | |
| 9. | |
| 10. | |
| 11. | |
| 12. | |
| 13. | |
| 14. | |
| 15. | |
| 16. | |
| 17. | |
| 18. | |
| 19. | |
| 20. | |

## ∼ 2 ∼
# MY 12 MONTH GOALS
The Clearer Your Goal, The Greater Your Faith.  *- MIKE MURDOCK*

| | DATE | GOALS |
|---|---|---|
| 1. | | |
| 2. | | |
| 3. | | |
| 4. | | |
| 5. | | |
| 6. | | |
| 7. | | |
| 8. | | |
| 9. | | |
| 10. | | |
| 11. | | |
| 12. | | |

## ∼ 3 ∼
# MY SCHEDULE & SUCCESS SHEET
"...that I may *daily* perform my vows" (Psalm 61:8).

| | *My Schedule* | *My Success* |
|---|---|---|
| 7:00 am | | |
| 8:00 am | | |
| 9:00 am | | |
| 10:00 am | | |
| 11:00 am | | |
| 12:00 noon | | |
| 1:00 pm | | |
| 2:00 pm | | |
| 3:00 pm | | |
| 4:00 pm | | |
| 5:00 pm | | |
| 6:00 pm | | |
| 7:00 pm | | |
| 8:00 pm | | |

# 4
# HOW TO TAKE NOTES

| TOPIC | THOUGHT |
|---|---|
| January 16, 2001<br>The Secret Place<br>*Numbers 23:19 | Memory Scripture of the Day.<br>"God is not a man, that He should lie; neither the son of man, that He should repent:  hath He said, and shall He not do it?" |
| Psalms 123-150<br>Proverbs 1-12 | My 40 Chapters in the Word. |
| Law of the Seed<br>Law of the Harvest | "They that sow in tears shall reap in joy.  He that goeth forth and weepeth, bearing precious seed, shall doubtless come again with rejoicing, bringing his sheaves with him" (Psalm 126:5-6). |
| Children | ...are an heritage of the Lord.<br>...are a reward from God to parents.<br>...were intended to be a source of great joy.  (Psalms 127:3-5; 128:3) |
| Job | *Your job and career should be a* Happiness *source of great joy and provision.* "For thou shalt eat the labour of thine hands:  happy shalt thou be, and it shall be well with thee."  (Psalm 128:2) |
| Prosperity | (Psalm 145:15-16) |
| Word of God | Everything created by God is used to fulfill and carry out His Word.  "Fire, and hail; snow, and vapours; stormy wind fulfilling His Word," (Psalm 148:8). |
| Wisdom<br>  Relationship<br><br>  Favor<br><br><br><br><br><br><br><br>  Health<br><br>  Promotion | ...is the most important thing on earth.  (Proverbs 4:7)<br>...delivers us from wrong people.  (Proverbs 2:12,16)<br>...determines longevity.  (Proverbs 3:2)<br>...determines favor.  (Proverbs 3:4)<br>...determines wealth.  (Proverbs 3:16)<br>...creates peace.  (Proverbs 3:17)<br>...is the instrument of creativity used by God in creating the universe.  (Proverbs 3:19)<br>...brings protection.  (Proverbs 3:21-22)<br>...prevents backsliding.  (Proverbs 3:23)<br>...affects our health.  (Proverbs 3:24)<br>...removes fear.  (Proverbs 3:24-25)<br>...is the key to promotion and honor.  (Proverbs 4:7-9) |
| Law of the Seed | *God commanded us to sow good Seed in every person possible around us.* "Withhold not good from them to whom it is due, when it is in the power of thine hand to do it" (Proverbs 3:27). |
| Passion for the Word | (Proverbs 7:1-3) |
| Fear of the Lord | ...is the beginning of Wisdom<br>...and knowledge.  (Proverbs 9:10; 1:7) |

| Topic | Thought |
|-------|---------|
|       |         |
|       |         |
|       |         |
|       |         |
|       |         |
|       |         |
|       |         |
|       |         |
|       |         |
|       |         |
|       |         |
|       |         |
|       |         |
|       |         |
|       |         |
|       |         |
|       |         |
|       |         |
|       |         |
|       |         |

# ∽ 5 ∽

# 12 INGREDIENTS OF THE PERFECT DAY

"But the path of the just is as the shining light, that shineth more and more unto *The Perfect Day*" (Proverbs 4:18).

1. **Preparation**...Of Your Mind, Spirit And Body.
2. **Meditation**...On The Law Of God, Our Wisdom.
3. **Motivation**...The Stirring Up Of Passion And Enthusiasm For Your Assignment.
4. **Organization**...Of Daily Schedule Of Appointments.
5. **Elimination**...Of Any Appointment Or Request That Does Not Qualify For Your Focus.
6. **Delegation**...Of Tasks To Others.
7. **Impartation**...From Your Mentors And To Protegés.
8. **Vocation**...The Problem You Are Assigned To Solve.
9. **Information**...The Pursuit Of Wisdom And Knowledge.
10. **Celebration**...Of Family And Those You Love.
11. **Documentation**...Journal Of Your Daily Experiences.
12. **Restoration**...Of Health Through Exercise And Sleep.

## YOUR DAILY SUCCESS ROUTINE

1. Perfect Your Daily Success Routine. The Secret Of Your Future Is Hidden In Your Daily Routine.
2. Set A Specific Prayer Time In Your Secret Place To Meet With The Holy Spirit.
3. Listen Continually For The Voice Of Your Mentor, The Holy Spirit.
4. Write Your Daily Goals Down Every Day.
5. Document And Visualize Your Dreams And Goals.
6. Always Keep 25% Of Your Day Unscheduled To Allow For Unexpected Interruptions.

**RECOMMENDED BOOKS AND TAPES:**
B-44      31 Secrets For Career Success (Book/114 pages/$10)
B-99      Secrets Of The Richest ManWho Ever Lived (Book/179 pages/$10)
TS-25    Secrets Of The Richest Man Who Ever Lived (6 Tapes/$30)

| Topic | Thought |
|---|---|
|  |  |
|  |  |
|  |  |
|  |  |
|  |  |
|  |  |
|  |  |
|  |  |
|  |  |
|  |  |
|  |  |
|  |  |
|  |  |
|  |  |
|  |  |
|  |  |
|  |  |
|  |  |
|  |  |
|  |  |
|  |  |
|  |  |
|  |  |
|  |  |
|  |  |
|  |  |
|  |  |
|  |  |
|  |  |

# 6
# 31 FACTS ABOUT WISDOM

1. Wisdom Is The Master Key To All The Treasures Of Life. (2 Chronicles 1:7-8,10-12; Colossians 2:2,3)
2. Wisdom Is A Gift From God To You. (2 Samuel 2:3; Proverbs 2:6; Daniel 2:21; Ephesians 2:17; 1 Corinthians 12:8)
3. The Fear Of God Is The Beginning Of Wisdom. (Job 28:28; Psalm 111:10; Proverbs 9:10)
4. Jesus Is Made Unto Us Wisdom. (1 Corinthians 1:30; Ephesians 1:5,8,17)
5. The Holy Spirit Is The Spirit Of Wisdom That Unleashes Your Gifts. (Exodus 31:1,3-4; 36:1; Daniel 1:4)
6. The Word Of God Is Able To Make You Wise Unto Salvation. (Psalm 107:43; John 5:39; 2 Timothy 3:15)
7. The Wisdom Of God Is Foolishness To The Natural Mind. (Proverbs 18:2; Isaiah 55:8-9; 1 Corinthians 2:4-5)
8. Your Conversation Reveals How Much Wisdom You Possess. (1 Kings 10:24; Proverbs 18:21; 29:11; James 3:2)
9. The Wisdom Of This World Is A False Substitute For The Wisdom Of God. (1 Corinthians 2:4,13; James 3:13-17)
10. All The Treasures Of Wisdom And Knowledge Are Hid In Jesus Christ. (1 Corinthians 1:23-24; 2:7-8; Colossians 2:2-3)
11. The Word Of God Is Your Source Of Wisdom. (Deuteronomy 4:5-6; Psalm 119:98-100; Proverbs 2:6)
12. God Will Give You Wisdom When You Take The Time To Listen. (Proverbs 2:6; Isaiah 40:31; John 10:27; James 1:5)
13. Right Relationships Increase Your Wisdom. (Proverbs 13:20; 1 Corinthians 15:33; 2 Thessalonians 3:6; 1 Timothy 6:5)
14. The Wisdom Of Man Is Foolishness To God. (1 Corinthians 1:20-21,25; 3:19)
15. Men Of Wisdom Will Always Be Men Of Mercy. (Galatians 6:1; James 3:17; 5:19-20)
16. Wisdom Is Better Than Jewels Or Money. (Job 28:18; Proverbs 3:13-15; 8:11; 16:16)
17. Wisdom Is More Powerful Than Weapons Of War. (Proverbs 12:6; Ecclesiastes 9:18; Isaiah 33:6; Acts 6:10)
18. The Mantle Of Wisdom Makes You 10 Times Stronger Than Those Without It. (Psalm 91:7; Ecclesiastes 7:19; Daniel 1:17,20)
19. The Wise Hate Evil...The Evil Hate The Wise. (Proverbs 1:7,22; 8:13; 9:8; 18:2)
20. Wisdom Reveals The Treasure In Yourself. (Proverbs 19:8; Ephesians 2:10; Philippians 1:6; 1 Peter 2:9-10)
21. The Proof Of Wisdom Is The Presence Of Joy And Peace. (Psalm 119:165; Proverbs 3:13; Ecclesiastes 7:12; James 3:17)
22. Wisdom Makes Your Enemies Helpless Against You. (Proverbs 16:7; Ecclesiastes 7:12; Isaiah 54:17; Luke 21:15)

23. Wisdom Creates Currents Of Favor And Recognition Toward You. (Proverbs 3:1,4; 4:8; 8:34-35)
24. The Wise Welcome Correction. (Proverbs 3:11-12; 9:8-9)
25. When The Wise Speak, Healing Flows. (Proverbs 10:11, 20-21; 12:18)
26. When You Increase Your Wisdom, You Will Increase Your Wealth. (Psalm 112:1,3; Proverbs 3:16; 8:18,21; 14:24)
27. Wisdom Can Be Imparted By The Laying On Of Hands Of A Man Of God. (Deuteronomy 34:9; Acts 6:6,8,10; 2 Timothy 1:6,14)
28. Wisdom Guarantees Promotion. (Proverbs 4:8-9; 8:15-16; Ezra 7:25)
29. Wisdom Loves Those Who Love Her. (Proverbs 2:3-5; 8:17,21)
30. He That Wins Souls Is Wise. (Proverbs 11:30; Daniel 12:3; Romans 10:14-15)
31. Wisdom Will Be Given To You When You Pray For It In Faith. (Matthew 7:7-8, 11; James 1:5-6)

# My Wisdom Notes

| Topic | Thought |
|---|---|
|  |  |
|  |  |
|  |  |
|  |  |
|  |  |
|  |  |
|  |  |
|  |  |
|  |  |
|  |  |
|  |  |
|  |  |
|  |  |

**RECOMMENDED BOOKS AND TAPES:**
B-01    Wisdom For Winning (Book/228 pages/$10)
TS-01   Wisdom For Winning (6 Tapes/$30)
B-40    Wisdom For Crisis Times (Book/112 pages/$9)
TS-40   Wisdom For Crisis Times (6 Tapes/$30)
B-99    Secrets Of The Richest Man Who Ever Lived (Book/179 pages/$10)
TS-25   Secrets Of The Richest Man Who Ever Lived (6 Tapes/$30)

# ≈ 7 ≈

# 31 WISDOM KEYS OF MIKE MURDOCK

1. Every Problem Is Always A Wisdom Problem.
2. When Your Heart Decides The Destination, Your Mind Will Design The Map To Reach It.
3. Whatever You Respect, You Will Attract.
4. The Secret Of Your Future Is Hidden In Your Daily Routine.
5. Your Rewards In Life Are Determined By The Kinds Of Problems You Are Willing To Solve For Others.
6. What You Make Happen For Others, God Will Make Happen For You.
7. An Uncommon Seed Always Creates An Uncommon Harvest.
8. The Word Of God Is The Wisdom Of God.
9. The Clearer Your Goals, The Greater Your Faith.
10. Your Focus Decides Your Feelings.
11. Your Self-Portrait Determines Your Self-Conduct.
12. Your Respect For Time Is A Prediction Of Your Financial Future.
13. Your Decisions Decide Your Wealth.
14. The Instruction You Follow Determines The Future You Create.
15. God's Only Pain Is To Be Doubted; God's Only Pleasure Is To Be Believed.
16. Your Goals Choose Your Mentors.
17. Your Success Is Decided By What You Are Willing To Ignore.
18. The Atmosphere You Create Determines The Product You Produce.
19. The Size Of Your Enemy Determines The Size Of Your Rewards.
20. Your Assignment Is Always The Problem God Has Designed You To Solve For Others.
21. What You Are Willing To Walk Away From Determines What God Will Bring To You.
22. Your Future Is Decided By Who You Choose To Believe.
23. Changes In Your Life Will Always Be Proportionate To Your Knowledge.
24. The Reward Of Pain Is The Willingness To Change.
25. Anything Permitted Increases.
26. Anything That Keeps Your Attention Has Become Your Master.
27. Your Life Is Whatever You Choose To Remember.
28. When You Want Something You Have Never Had, You Must Do Something You Have Never Done.
29. What You Repeatedly Hear, You Eventually Believe.
30. All Men Fall; The Great Ones Get Back Up.
31. You Cannot Correct What You Are Unwilling To Confront.

*Excerpts from The Wisdom Key Devotional B-165 (Book/60 pages/$8)
– Also available in Spanish SB-165
*Wisdom Keys Of Mike Murdock CD series CDPAK-02 (4 CDs/4 Books for $40)

| Topic | Thought |
|-------|---------|
|  |  |

# 8
# 31 FACTS ABOUT THE HOLY SPIRIT

1. The Holy Spirit Is A Person, Not A Dove, Wind Or Fire. (John 14:16)
2. The Holy Spirit Created You. (Job 33:4)
3. The Holy Spirit Is The Author Of All Scripture And The Inspiration Of All Scripture. (2 Timothy 3:16)
4. The Holy Spirit Confirms That Jesus Is Within You. (1 John 4:13)
5. The Holy Spirit Decides The Skills, Gifts And Talents Within You. (1 Corinthians 12:4- 11)
6. The Holy Spirit Gives Life. (2 Corinthians 3:6)
7. The Holy Spirit Confirms You Are A Child Of God. (Romans 8:16)
8. The Holy Spirit Imparts A Personal Prayer Language That Dramatically Increases Your Strength And Faith. (Jude 1:20)
9. The Holy Spirit Talks To You. (Revelation 2:7)
10. The Holy Spirit Reveals The Truth You Need To Live Victoriously. (John 16:13)
11. The Holy Spirit Is The Source Of The Anointing...The Special Power Of God Given For Your Assignment. (Luke 4:18)
12. The Holy Spirit Is The Source Of Every Desired Emotion You Are Pursuing In Your Life. (Galatians 5:22-23)
13. The Holy Spirit Knows Every Detail Of The Purpose And Plan Of God For Your Life. (Romans 8:27-28)
14. The Holy Spirit Decides When You Are Ready To Be Tested. (Luke 4:1-2)
15. The Holy Spirit Is Your Intercessor On Earth. (Romans 8:26)
16. The Holy Spirit Loves Singing. (Psalm 100:1-2)
17. The Holy Spirit Is The Source Of Your Joy. (Psalm 16:11)
18. The Holy Spirit Is Your Only Source Of True Peace. (Galatians 5:22-23; Philippians 4:7)
19. The Holy Spirit Removes All Fear. (2 Timothy 1:7)
20. The Holy Spirit Shows You Pictures Of Your Future. (John 16:13; Acts 7:55)
21. The Holy Spirit Gives You The Necessary Love You Need Towards Others. (Romans 5:5)
22. The Holy Spirit Decides Your Assignment. (Acts 13:2-4)
23. The Holy Spirit Enables You To Enter Into The Kingdom Of God. (John 3:5-6)
24. The Holy Spirit Only Guides Those Who Are Sons Of God. (Romans 8:14)
25. The Holy Spirit Knows The Person To Whom You Have Been Assigned. (Acts 8:29)
26. The Holy Spirit Will Send Inner Warnings To Protect You From Wrong People And Places. (Acts 16:6-7)
27. The Holy Spirit Is Grieved And Saddened By Wrong Conduct. (Ephesians 4:30-31)
28. The Holy Spirit Critiques Every Moment, Motive And Movement Of Your Life. (Jer. 17:10)
29. The Holy Spirit Becomes An Enemy To The Rebellious. (Isaiah 63:10)
30. The Holy Spirit Withdraws When Offended. (Ephesians 4:30-32; Hosea 5:15)
31. The Holy Spirit Raised Jesus From The Dead, And He Will Raise You From The Dead When Christ Returns To The Earth. (Romans 8:11)

| Topic | Thought |
|-------|---------|
|       |         |

# 9
## 31 Facts About Your Assignment

1. Everything God Created Was Created To Solve A Problem.
2. Your Assignment Is Always To A Person Or A People.
3. Your Assignment Is Not Your Decision, But Your *Discovery*.
4. What You Hate Is A Clue To Something You Are Assigned To *Correct*.
5. What *Grieves* You Is A Clue To Something You Are Assigned To *Heal*.
6. What You Love Is A Clue To The Gifts, Skills And *Wisdom* You Contain.
7. Your Assignment Is *Geographical*.
8. Your Assignment Will Take You Where You Are *Celebrated* Instead Of Tolerated.
9. Your Assignment Is Your Significant Difference From Others.
10. If You Rebel Against Your Assignment, God May Permit Painful Experiences To Correct You.
11. What You Love Most Is A Clue To Your Assignment.
12. God Can Forgive Any Sin Or Mistake You Have Made In Pursuit Of Your Assignment.
13. Your Assignment Will Require *Seasons Of Preparation*.
14. Your Assignment May Contain *Seasons Of Insignificance*.
15. Your Assignment May Require *Seasons Of Waiting*.
16. Your Assignment May Require *Seasons Of Isolation*.
17. You Are The Only One God Has Anointed For Your Specific Assignment.
18. People Will Be Assigned By Hell To Distract, Delay, Discourage And Derail Your Assignment.
19. Your Assignment May Sometimes Seem To Be In Vain.
20. Your Assignment Will Require Miracles.
21. Your Assignment Will Require Your *Total Focus*.
22. You Must Only Attempt A God-Given And God-Approved Assignment.
23. You Will Only Succeed When Your Assignment Becomes An Obsession.
24. Your Assignment Requires *Planning*.
25. Your Assignment Will Be Revealed *Progressively*.
26. Intercessors Can Determine The Outcome Of Your Assignment.
27. Someone Is Always Observing You Who Is Capable Of Greatly Blessing You In Your Assignment.
28. Your Assignment May Require Unusual And Unwavering Trust In A Man Or Woman Of God.
29. The Problem That *Infuriates* You The Most Is Often The Problem God Has Assigned You To Solve.
30. Your Assignment May Seem Small, Yet Be The Golden Link In A Great Chain Of Miracles.
31. Your Assignment Is The Only Place Financial Provision Is Guaranteed.

*Excerpts from the four volume series of:
    The Assignment, Vols. 1-4 (paperbacks $10 each)
    The Assignment, (6 Tapes) TS-52/$30

| Topic | Thought |
|---|---|
|  |  |

# 31 FACTS ABOUT THE LAW OF THE SEED

1. There Will Never Be A Day In Your Life That You Have Nothing To Sow.
2. You Will Always Reap What You Sow.
3. Seed-Faith Is Sowing What You Have Been Given To Create What You Have Been Promised.
4. Your Seed Is Anything That Blesses Somebody.
5. The Law Of The Seed (Sowing And Reaping) Was Intended To Birth Encouragement, Hope And Excitement Toward A Harvest.
6. Your Seed Is Any Tool God Has Given You To Create Your Future.
7. Something You Have Been Given By God Will Create Anything Else You Have Been Promised By God.
8. You Are A Walking Collection Of Seeds.
9. Someone Near You Is "The Soil" Qualified To Receive Your Seed.
10. When You Let Go Of What Is In Your Hand, God Will Let Go Of What Is In His Hand.
11. Everything You Possess Is Something You Have Been Given.
12. If You Keep What You Presently Have, That Is The Most It Will Ever Be.
13. When You Ask God For A Harvest, God Will Always Ask You For A Seed.
14. Your Seed Is The Only Proof You Have Mastered Greed.
15. When You Increase The Size Of Your Seed, You Increase The Size Of Your Harvest.
16. A Seed Of Nothing Always Schedules A Season Of Nothing.
17. Your Seed Must Always Be Comparable To The Harvest You Are Desiring.
18. Every Seed Contains An Invisible Instruction.
19. Your Seed Is Always Your Door Out Of Trouble.
20. When You Give Your Seed An Assignment, You Are Giving Your Faith An Instruction.
21. Nothing Leaves Heaven Until Something Leaves Earth.
22. Your *Seed* Is *What* God Multiplies; Your *Faith* Is *Why* He Multiplies It.
23. When You Sow Into Others What Nobody Else Is Willing To Sow, You Will Reap What No One Else Has Ever Reaped.
24. Your Seed Is The Only Influence You Have Over Your Future.
25. Your Seed Is The Only Master Your Future Will Obey.
26. The Seed Of Forgiveness Into Others, Creates The Harvest Of Mercy From Others.
27. What You *Keep* Is Your Harvest, What You *Sow* Is Your Seed.
28. When God Talks To You About A Seed, He Has A Harvest On His Mind.
29. The Seed That Leaves Your Hand Never Leaves Your Life; It Just Leaves Your Hand And Enters Into Your Future Where It Multiplies.
30. Your Seed Is A Photograph Of Your Faith.
31. An Uncommon Seed Always Creates An Uncommon Harvest.

*Excerpts from 31 Reasons People Do Not Receive Their Financial Harvest

| Topic | Thought |
|-------|---------|
|       |         |

# ❧ 11 ❧

## 31 THINGS GOD WANTS TO INCREASE IN YOUR LIFE

1. God Wants To Increase *The Miracles* You Experience. (Mark 11:23,24)
2. God Wants To Increase *Your Revelation* Of The Holy Spirit In Your Life. (Psalm 25:12-14; John 14:15-16)
3. God Wants To Increase *Your Wisdom*. (Proverbs 4:7; James 1:5; Ephesians 1:8)
4. God Wants To Increase *Your Finances*. (Psalm 112:1,3)
5. God Wants To Increase *Your Life* Span On The Earth. (Ephesians 6:2-3; Psalm 92:14)
6. God Wants To Increase *Your Love* For Others. (1 John 2:5; Romans 5:5)
7. God Wants To Increase *Your Joy*. (John 15:11-12)
8. God Wants To Increase *The Fruit* You Produce. (Colossians 1:12)
9. God Wants *Your Strength* To Increase. (Colossians 1:11)
10. God Wants To Increase The *Flow Of Blessings* Into Your Life. (Deuteronomy 28:1-14)
11. God Wants To Increase *Your Victories* Over Your Enemies. (Deuteronomy 28:7)
12. God Wants To Increase *Your Endurance* Ability. (Acts 5:41)
13. God Wants To Increase *Your Peace*. (Philippians 4:7)
14. God Wants To Increase *Your Gratitude And Thankfulness* Toward Him. (1 Thess. 5:18)
15. God Wants To Increase *Your Intercession And Prayer Life*. (1 Thessalonians 5:17)
16. God Wants To Increase *Your Healing And Health*. (Isaiah 58:8)
17. God Wants To Increase *Your Soul-Winning*. (Mark 16:15; Proverbs 11:30)
18. God Wants To Increase *The Flow Of Favor* Into Your Life. (Psalm 5:12)
19. God Wants To Increase *The Laughter And Shouting* In Your Life. (Psalm 98:4)
20. God Wants To Increase *The Protection* Around You. (Psalm 91:10-11)
21. God Wants To Increase *Your Achievements*. (Ephesians 3:20)
22. God Wants To Increase *His Power* In Your Life. (Acts 1:8)
23. God Wants To Increase *Your Pleasure And Enjoyment* In His World. (Psalm 36:8-9)
24. God Wants To Increase *Your Rest And Relaxation*. (Psalm 37:7)
25. God Wants To Increase *The Fear Of God* In Your Life. (Proverbs 9:10)
26. God Wants To Increase *The Good You Are Doing* Towards Others. (Proverbs 3:27)
27. God Wants To Increase *Your Self-Confidence* In Accomplishing Your Assignment. (Prov. 3:25-26)
28. God Wants To Increase *The Time You Spend In The Secret Place* With Him. (Psalm 27:4)
29. God Wants To Increase *Your Integrity And Purity*. (Psalm 25:21)
30. God Wants To Increase *The Forgiveness* You Sow Into Others. (Luke 6:38)
31. God Wants To Increase *Your Sowing* So Your Reaping Can Increase. (2 Corinthians 9:6)

*Excerpts from 7 Keys To 1000 Times More
   B-104 (Book/128 pages/$10)
   TS-30 (6 Tapes/$30)
   V116 (Video/$30)

| Topic | Thought |
|-------|---------|
|       |         |

# ❧ 12 ❧
# 8 LEVELS OF SEED-SOWING; MY PERSONAL TESTIMONY
## HONORING THE INTERNAL VOICE OF THE HOLY SPIRIT

*Your Seed Is The Only Influence You Have Over Your Future.*

I once asked Brother Oral Roberts, What his greatest revelation received from God had been. His response... "Seed-Faith, sowing a Seed for an *expected* result or Harvest."

Oral Robert's own faith in God is legendary. His own revelation of The Holy Spirit has affected my life radically. Brother Robert's understanding of the *Law of the Seed* has revolutionized the prosperity of millions. Only eternity will reveal the countless miracles that have happened because of his faith in God.

Throughout the years, I have experienced different levels of Seed sowing by *honoring the internal Voice of The Holy Spirit.* Many Wisdom Keys have been birthed through my experiences in Seed-Faith giving.

The faith of thousands has been unleashed through the teaching about *The Seed* and *the expectation of a Harvest.* My *hatred* of poverty and my *passion* to see the body of Christ receive the Harvest God desires for them is a driving force in my life. The following is a brief account of my experiences in Seed-Faith.

## *8 LEVELS OF THE SEED*

**1** *Seed of $58...Craziest Instruction God Ever Gave Me.*
*Something You Have Been Given Will Create Anything Else You Have Been Promised.*
It was in Washington, DC, on the platform of Miracle Faith Center when God spoke to me to plant a $58 Seed representing the 58 kinds of blessings I had researched. I was to sow the Seed as a monument to my faith that the 58 kinds of blessings would occur during my lifetime. It sounded ridiculous to me...I did not even like odd numbers. Immediately, I wrote out the Seed for $58. Then, The Holy Spirit whispered again, to plant a $58 Seed for my son, who at that time was living with his mother. I had spent thousands of dollars in legal fees to gain custody of my son. After planting the $58 Seed, I returned home within a few weeks to find my secretary at the airport with the news...my son would be arriving in one hour. His mother had decided he could spend the rest of his life with me.

I was in a church in Houston on a Sunday night and The Holy Spirit said, "Tell them about your $58 Seed miracle." I said, "Lord, that is crazy...this is too weird." He said, "Tell them what I did for you." So, I told the people, "If you never do it again, plant a Seed tonight for $58, count off 58 days and see what God will do."

*Transcribed from a LIVE service while Dr. Murdock was sharing his testimonies.

A young man walked up after church and said, "I hope this thing works." I asked, "Why?" He said, "I will be evicted from my house if I do not have $745 by Wednesday." I asked, "Did you sow the $58 Seed?" He said, "I did." I said, "Well, I would expect a miracle." In about ten minutes, he came running back into the church screaming and shouting, "It works."

He was sitting in his car ready to leave the parking lot after we had talked. A woman walked up, knocked on his car window and asked, "Are you asking God for a miracle?" He said, "Yes ma'am, I am." She asked, "How much?" He said, "I need $745 by Wednesday." She said, "When you walked by me, The Holy Spirit told me to write you a check for whatever you needed." She wrote him a check in the parking lot within ten minutes after he sowed a $58 Seed.

A young man who traveled with me, heard me tell about the $58 Seed. He came up after the service that night and said, "I planted a $58 Seed." He had not seen two of his girls, eight and thirteen years old, in five years. His mother and father were not saved. His daddy was 86 years old...had never given his life to Christ. He had a sister who left home 48 years before...he had never even seen her. They did not know whether she was alive or dead.

In 14 days, he got to spend one week with his two daughters. Two of his sisters were saved. His mother was saved, and his 86 year old father was saved. Within 21 days after sowing his Seed, his sister, whom he had not heard from in 48 years, was miraculously located in Irving, Texas. He had a family reunion and flew her back home...all this, from a $58 Seed.

## My Mother And Father's Harvest From A $58 Seed

I sent my mother and father a tape and said, "If you never do it again, plant a $58 Seed and count off 58 days and see what God will do." I knew my mother needed a miracle...she had a $48,000 doctor bill at St. Luke's Episcopal Hospital for double by-pass heart surgery valve replacement...not a penny of medical insurance. They emptied their life savings and got the bill down to $26,622. She sowed the $58 Seed.

In 21 days, my phone rings. There were three messages on my phone. I came in and called home. My father got on one line and my mother got on the other line. My dad's first words were, "Son, I can hardly catch my breath. We got a letter from the hospital...We have been on the phone with them. They said, 'Your bill of $26,622 just came to our attention. Once in a while we want to do something good for somebody. We have decided to mark it *paid in full*.'" They paid my mother and father's doctor bill of $26,622 *just 21 days* after sowing a $58 Seed!

Since that time, thousands of believers have sown the $58 Seed, writing on their checks these words, "Covenant of 58 Blessings." Through following an instruction from a man of God, they have received a Harvest of family members being born again, healings, restored marriages and financial deliverances...all from *"the craziest instruction God ever gave me."*

# 2 Seed of $100...My First Uncommon Seed.

*The Seasons Of Your Life Will Change Every Time You Decide To Use Your Faith.*
In June of 1967, I was sitting on the fourth row, South Texas District Counsel of the Assemblies of God in Victoria, Texas. Charles Greenaway, an Assemblies of God missionary evangelist to Europe, was preaching. He began to talk about Leviticus 19:9-10, where the rich men were instructed to leave the corners of their fields for the poor. He made the statement, "The field is your income. The corner is your outgo. The bigger you make your corner, the bigger God will make your field." I thought he had made a mistake; I snickered to a friend that he had said the statement backwards. I had always told God, "If you will give me a bigger field, I will give you a bigger corner." However, he said if I would return the corner, God would enlarge my field. He was a cocky, almost an arrogant style preacher. He said, "In Malachi 3, when God says throw Me the Seed to prove Me, it is the only scriptural place where God told you to prove His existence." God said, "Throw me a Seed. If more comes back, that is the proof I am here."

Let me remind you, I had always paid my tithe. We were taught, you had better pay your tithe or God's curse will be on you. So we tithed...not cheerfully. I could not tell you how many times I paid the tithe and thought, "There went a shirt." I understand the non-tither mindset, because we do not necessarily get a reward quickly from the tithe. It is the Law of Eventuality. It is the only way God can document trust. Tithe is not an exchange. *It is an investment.*

I am a *dare devil* kind of guy. Brother Greenaway made this statement, "I dare you to prove God." I was sitting on the fourth row listening. I had a 1953 Chevrolet. One month, my income was $35. One month it was $90. My house cost $150 for the *entire* house. I had never, to my knowledge, heard anything like that.

Something leaped inside me. People were standing and giving what he called *faith promises*. He basically explained that if you had faith to believe that God would give you the Seed, you promised to give it back to Him if He provided it.

> You can only *live* the part of the Gospel you *hear*. You can only *understand* the part of the Gospel that is *explained*. You can *never* rise above your persuasion. *You are living what you have been taught.*

This does not sound big today, but when you are twenty years old and your income is less than $3,000 a year, and you live in a house that cost $150, and you are holding your car door shut because the latch is broken, you are willing to prove anything. So I stood to my feet, shaking, and pledged $100. The reason...because he said I had a year to sow the Seed. So, I had a year to *work with my faith.*

Now that sounds like nothing to me now, but it is like working with muscles...you work with what you *have* got until you get what you *have not*. You work with your *faith level.*

I was driving home nervous. All I could think about from Victoria, Texas, to Lake Charles, Louisiana, was, "Where on earth am I going to get $100? Where on earth am I going to get $100?" Those were the days when people would give me a dollar wrapped around two quarters. That $1.50 was a $1.00's worth of gas and a loaf of bread.

The following Sunday, Merle Dailey, a former pianist for the old Stamps Quartet, was going through town and stopped at my dad's church. My dad had him to play a piano solo. He got through playing on my dad's Steinway piano and stood...I can still see him standing there with his hands in his pockets. He was about fifty-five years old. He said, "God has been so good to me. My pockets are full of $100 bills." I had never heard of anybody having a $100 bill, much less a guy bragging on it and telling all of us his pockets were full. Suddenly he stopped and looked over at me and said, "God just told me to give Mike one of them."

The next morning, I deposited the money and sent my $100 faith promise to the South Texas District Council Assemblies of God.

Tuesday, I was driving to Beeville, Texas for revival at the First Assembly of God church. Going through town, I saw a little luggage trailer: "For Sale $100." It was exactly the kind of luggage trailer I had been looking for to hold my luggage, clothes, etc. It was like the enemy said, "See what you could have bought had you not paid your *faith promise*."

I was playing the old upright piano before church began that night. A lady and a man walked in. I did not know them at the time. They gave me a check for $150. *I was ecstatic.* I had enough to buy the trailer plus extra. The next day I went and bought the trailer for $100 and had $50 left over and sent it immediately to the South Texas District Council Assemblies of God. You may be thinking, "You already paid your faith promise." I am not stupid. Anything that was working *this good...this fast*, I was going to work the living daylights out of it.

The next night, I was playing the piano again before church. I always played before church to sort of "get myself acclimated." The same couple walked in again. She walked up and said, "We could not sleep last night. God told us to buy that trailer for you, too." She handed me another check for $100.

Now understand this...I was sowing at a $100 level and I was reaping at a $100 level. Now I have learned since then, that if I sow $100, I do not receive a $10,000 check as a hundredfold return; I get a collection of $100's. *Whatever you faith out, that is the level you faith back.*

From there, I went on to Central Assembly of God church in San Antonio Texas. Sunday night, I was playing the piano at the close of the service. We were having an altar call. A man came up behind me and said gruffly, "Here." The people were singing. I turned around and he shoved something in my hand. I opened it, and it was a $100 bill. Notice, I was *faithing* out $100 and I was receiving $100. *I was ecstatic.* I turned to him and said, "Brother, thank you." In my mind, I can still see him. He turned to me and said, "Don't thank me. When God tells you to do something, you have to go ahead and do it." That was the first time I understood Luke 6:38, "I will *cause* men to give to you." People that do not even *want* to give to you *will* give to you.

# 3 Seed of $200...What You Are Willing To Walk Away From Determines What God Will Bring To You.

Eventually, I was so blessed I had two $100 bills. Again, I was ecstatic. I had money tucked away in my wallet to go buy some clothes.

I went to hear a minister friend who was preaching in Lake Charles. While I was sitting there, The Holy Spirit said, "Plant your two $100 bills into his ministry." Of course, I explained to the Lord, I was going to buy some clothes so that I could look good for the ministry. Yet, I was obedient to sow the Seed.

Seven nights later at midnight, I received a call from a couple outside of Memphis, Tennessee whose son had died. A year earlier, I had been in the church where they attended. They said that God had spoken to them to treat me as their son...they wanted to buy me some clothes. They asked if I was coming through Memphis any time soon. *Yes, I was!*

They brought me to the nicest men's store and bought me four suits, shirts and ties.

Six months later, they bought me *four more*.
Six months later, they bought me *four more*.
Six months later, they bought me *four more*.
Six months later, they bought me *four more*.
*Six months later, they bought me four more.*

On a Sunday night, I went to hear a pastor friend. He stopped the service half-way through and said, "I see Mike Murdock at the back." He said, "Son, God just spoke to me to stop the service and receive an offering to buy you some clothes."

On a Wednesday night, I went to hear another minister friend and his wife. While I was sitting in the service, he said, "I see Mike Murdock. We have never met, but I have seen you in conferences. God just spoke to me to receive an offering to buy you some clothes."

Some months later, a long-time lady minister friend, called, and asked me to come over to her home. When I arrived, there were clothes from one end of the room to the other end of the room. I asked, "What are all these clothes?" She said, "God told me to buy you some clothes."

A pastor friend in Louisville, Kentucky, leaned over one night while we were in church. He asked, "What are you doing tomorrow?" I replied, "What would you like to do?" He said, "God told me to buy you some clothes."

A pastor friend in New York, Chaplin to the baseball players, leaned over on a Sunday night and asked, "What are you doing tomorrow?" My response, "What would you like to do?" He said, "God told me to buy you some clothes."

The next day, we were in New York picking out clothes, and into the shop walked another minister friend of mine and asked, "What are you doing...buying Mike some clothes?" My friend said, "Yes." He said, "Well, I might as well buy him some, too."

Later, I was in Hong Kong in a clothing store selecting custom suits and special printed clothes...special kinds of shirts. A couple of my minister friends walked in the store. They asked, "Are you buying some clothes?" I said, "Yes." I pulled out my credit card and they said, "We are not going to let you pay for any of these clothes. We have to pay for these clothes."

I could not tell you how many people from Houston to Chicago, and everywhere else I go, who place their business cards in my hand and ask, "Would you please let me take you shopping to buy you some clothes?"

I have received an "on going" Harvest of clothes through the obedience to plant a $200 Seed.

This level of Seed-sowing is where I received the Wisdom Key: *What You Are Willing To Walk Away From Determines What God Will Bring To You.* I walked away from my "clothes money," and God has abundantly supplied my clothes.

## 4 Seed of $1,000...Where I Broke The Back Of Poverty.
*When You Let Go Of What Is In Your Hand, God Will Let Go Of What Is In His Hand.*

I broke the back of poverty with a $1,000 Seed. It happened on a telethon. I had just received a royalty check of $5,000 for my song-writing. At the time, sheets were tacked over my windows...I wanted draperies so badly. I needed a kitchen table and chairs...I had nothing. I had wonderful plans for my $5,000. *It was my Harvest.*

Suddenly The Holy Spirit spoke to me to plant $1,000. I explained to The Holy Spirit that I was going to buy draperies and a kitchen table with chairs. It took forty-five minutes for me to fully obey. The next day, The Holy Spirit spoke again: I planted a second Seed of $1,000 as a covenant for my son.

The following Sunday morning, The Holy Spirit spoke the third time to plant a $1,000 at a church in Dallas. That afternoon, kneeling in the pastor's office, I prayed, "Holy Spirit, five days ago I had $5,000. Within the last five days, You have spoken to me to plant three Seeds of $1,000. If this is not You and Your plan, stop me now!" The Holy Spirit gave me another Wisdom Key: *When God Talks To You About A Seed, He Has A Harvest On His Mind.*

That afternoon, He gave me several other Wisdom Keys:
▶ *Nothing Leaves Heaven Until Something Leaves The Earth.*
▶ *When You Open Your Hand, I Will Open My Windows.*
▶ *The Seed That Leaves Your Hand Never Leaves Your Life; It Enters Your Future Where It Multiplies.*

The miracles began.

That night after the service, a man walked up. He opened a book featuring rare automobiles. He explained the value of one of the cars and said, "There are only nineteen of these in the world. I happen to have Serial Number 1 – the first one they made. It is my pet car. *God told me to give it to you!*"

The next day, Monday morning, a man walked into my office. He said, "I understand you need a van for your ministry. Order the best one you can buy, and *I will pay for it.*"

Tuesday morning, the next day, a friend called me for lunch. As we sat at the restaurant, he explained that he could not sleep the previous night. The Holy Spirit kept speaking to him to give me a special Seed of $10,000! From that point his life was never the same.

Within a couple of years, almost $400,000 came into my life from song-writing royalties. *When God Talks To You About A Seed, He Has A Harvest On His Mind.*

I broke the back of poverty with a $1,000 Seed. *What You Can Walk Away From You Have Mastered; What You Cannot Walk Away From Has Mastered You.*

# 5 Seed of $8,500...The Lifetime Blessing.
*When You Want Something You Have Never Had, You Must Do Something You Have Never Done.*

Ruth so respected Boaz that everything he had came to her. (See Ruth 1-4).

Since my obedience to sow the $1,000 Seeds, I have prayed a "Boaz Anointing" over thousands of people who have been obedient to this level of Seed sowing—The prayer that every time God blesses *me*, He blesses *them*...every time God gives *me* a miracle, He gives *them* a miracle.

*We sow up for wealth*—Ezekiel 44:30...that when you give to the man of God, he will cause the blessing to rest on your house. *You sow down*, into those who are poor or below you financially, *for health*. (Read Psalm 41:1-3 and Isaiah 58:7-8). The greatest deception of poverty is that those who "*have*" are supposed to sponsor you. However, once you get a revelation of The Seed, *if* you will sow *up*, the blessing will come down from the priest of the house. You must sow into something *bigger than you* for the blessing to come *down to you*. If you lack, start sowing up instead of expecting those who are *up* to sow down. I have bought my father his houses and cars for the last thirty years. Why? He is my father, the priest over my home. *What You Make Happen For A Man Of God, God Will Make Happen For You.*

I had received a royalty check for $8,500, and was ecstatic. I am a professional shopper...I love shopping. I could not wait...$8,500!

It was on a Sunday night in Columbus, Ohio that I was preaching for a minister friend. The Holy Spirit said, "Do not receive an offering for your own ministry; receive an offering for their ministry." Well, that happens all the time to me, so that was not shocking. Then, The Holy Spirit whispered to me, "How would you like to explore and experiment with what I could do with your $8,500?" That is the way He presented it...because the opportunity to sow is not always a command. Sometimes it is *an invitation to an investment*. I thought, "*That is my Harvest.* Hallelujah, the devil is not going to get my Harvest." Then, The Holy Spirit said again, "How would you like to explore and experiment with what I could do with your $8,500?" Then I thought, "Is that all I will ever want? Is my dream $8,500? Is this my lifetime goal to have $8,500? No, my dream is bigger than $8,500." *If I want God in my future, I have to give Him a reason for being in my future.*

Now it took God a while to get the Seed from me. I hear pastors talk about hilarious giving, but when I give a large offering, I feel sick sometimes for days thinking, "I hope that was God." Yet, I gave the entire $8,500. I went back to the hotel room and plummeted into an indescribable depression. I literally could not talk for seven days.

At the end of the seven days, I cried out to God and said, "God, I did that because I thought You wanted me to give the $8,500. If I have missed You, I am so sorry." The devil had really worked me over saying, "That was not God. That was your imagination. You have preached 'giving' so much you cannot hold on to anything." God spoke one single sentence back to me...just one. He said, "Anything you do in an attempt to obey Me will not go unrewarded."

Six weeks afterwards, I was at the Hyatt Regency hotel, 7:15 in the morning walking back and forth praying in The Holy Spirit. Suddenly, God gave me an idea...I saw a Bible for business people, then The Mother's Topical Bible just for mothers. I saw one for fathers. I took a pen, and began to write down, The Mother's Topical Bible, The Father's Topical Bible, The Teenager's Topical Bible...The Businessman's Topical Bible.

I called a friend and the friend said, "That thing will sell. I will produce the product, put it in stores, and I will give you a percentage of everything I sell if you will give me the idea." I said, "It is yours. Take it." He signed contracts with Wal-Mart, K-Mart, and Hallmark. In a short time, there were $1.7 million in sales, and I received a percent of every book that sold. Every ninety days I started receiving a royalty check from that idea. With the first royalty check I was able to build a gymnasium at my house with an NBA basketball court. The second royalty check bought me a beautiful Rolls Royce, cash, black on black.

I received Christian Booksellers Association's list of the top one-hundred books in Christianity in reference and sales. Five of the first twenty were Mike Murdock's Topical Bibles. Nothing like that had ever been done previously.

*God gave me a lifetime income from a one-time Seed of $8,500.*

# 6 *Seed of $10,000*
*The Difference Between Seasons Is Simply An Instruction.*

I flew to preach for a pastor friend of mine...1,300 preachers at the First Assembly of God in New Orleans, Louisiana. I got up to preach that night, feeling anointed. I had received the $10,000 Harvest after sowing three $1,000 Seeds from my song-writing royalties. I was carrying the Harvest in my pocket...$10,000...*this works*.

At the close of the service, The Holy Spirit said, "Tell ten preachers to plant $10,000, and if they are obedient, I will open doors for them...open the windows of Heaven for them." I said, "God is going to speak to ten men here tonight to plant $10,000. If you will obey God, God will bless you."

Suddenly, I started feeling the *sickest* sensation. The Holy Spirit said, "I want you to plant the $10,000 I just gave you." I had already identified the $10,000 as my Harvest. It was *not* Seed. This was my *Harvest* from the $1,000 Seed.

I had everyone to keep praying while I was putting God through the test.
"This $10,000 is a *testimony*. I want to tell everybody what You gave me for the $1,000

Seed. If I give this $10,000, I will have nothing left. This is *my Harvest*. You have just blessed me. This is a testimony I want to give."

I gave the $10,000 Seed, and then thought, "What have I done? What have I done?" I do not think you will ever follow an illogical instruction that you do not later contest in your mind.

The next day, I got a phone call from a television minister. He said, "We want to run a program for you every week on television…free." That same week, another television minister called to make sure I would accept his offer. He said, "I am serious about that program I offered. I want to give you a free program if you will make it." Easily, I was offered a quarter of a million dollars worth of television airtime *within seven days* after sowing the $10,000 Seed.

# 7 *Seed of $25,000…Seed of Honor.*
*The Anointing You Respect Is The Anointing That Increases In Your Life.*

I was sitting with Oral Roberts at a meal and The Holy Spirit said, "Give him $25,000." I felt as though I had intercepted a memo that God was giving to Brother Roberts, to give *me* $25,000. The Holy Spirit repeated the instruction, "Plant a Seed of $25,000 into his life." I had already planted thousands of dollars into Oral Roberts' ministry. I was not in the mood to give any more. I actually was in the frame of mind to wait for the Harvest from the last Seed I had planted before planting again. Yet, I knew the voice of The Holy Spirit. I knew that *delayed obedience is rebellion*. So I said to Brother Roberts, "I will meet you at the hotel in an hour-and-a-half to give you a $25,000 Seed."

Within *seventy-two hours* Heaven opened on my life. Pastors called and ordered thousands of my books.

Within a few days, a friend sent me a video, "Happy birthday to you." I walked outside and there was a brand new black Corvette as a gift for my birthday.

A few weeks later, a woman whom I did not know, drove up. She said, "God told me to give you my Corvette, a special collection."

A few months later, I pulled up at my house, and there was another Corvette, a brand new, yellow convertible…a gift from a friend.

I was preparing to leave a hotel room one evening, when the phone rang and a friend said, "You have so changed my life, what could I do to bless you?" I answered, "I do not need anything. Just pray for my Wisdom." The friend asked, "What about a Rolex watch?" I said, "I have more watches than I need." He said, "What about a car?" I said, "I do not need a car. I have more cars than I can drive right now." The friend asked, "Have you seen the new BMW 745's?" I said, "Yes, but I do not need a car." He asked, "What color would you have if you had one?" I answered, "Black on black." It arrived fourteen days later, loaded, straight from Germany.

I had seized a moment of Uncommon Faith. *An Uncommon Seed Always Creates An Uncommon Harvest.*

# 8 Seed For A Debt-Free Home.

*Your Reaction To A Man Of God Determines God's Reaction To You.*

I was in Chicago for a conference. The pastor asked me to arrive a day early—which I never typically do because of time restraints. He said, "I just wish you would come one day early before you speak." I was sitting on the front row, and the preacher began to talk about the *precious* Seed. When he completed teaching his revelation, he said, "I want you to plant a Seed equal to one month's mortgage payment. Write on the bottom of the Seed, 'a debt-free house,' put it in your left hand, hit it three times and believe that God will give you a debt-free house in twelve months."

Well, anybody can be debt-free. The homeless are already debt-free. I can get you debt-free in an hour...*but a debt-free home?*

So, after I planted my Seed, I thought, "I want to put some *disclaimers* on this Seed. I do not want to use my CD's or savings account. I want You to do this supernaturally." It is called *water on the sacrifice*. (See 1 Kings 18:33-35.) "Let's see how hard I can make this. I want to get God to *really* show off His power."

I was obedient to the instruction of the man of God.

*I LIVE by the Seed.* If I cannot believe God regarding my Seed, what can I believe Him about? There is nothing more powerful than a person who can walk away from money, because money is the god of this world. That is what an offering is...a burial service for the god of this world. The Seed goes into the ground and it will produce a Harvest.

I still recall the words of Oral Roberts: "Next to Jesus, the most *sure thing* on earth is that *The Seed Will Multiply.*"

I did not know the day would come that I would buy houses with *cash*. I have a Jehovah-Jireh in my life. If people who drink, gamble, curse and hate the presence of God can reap a Harvest in God's world, how much more can those who call Him, "Father"?

My house was debt-free in eight months.

*When You Open Your Hands, God Will Open His Windows.*

### My Special Prayer For You Today:

"Holy Spirit, thank You first for placing men of God in my life who unlocked my faith. They saw You as a Provider when I had only known You as a Personal Savior and Baptizer. Your words in their mouth...transformed my Financial World. For that, I give You all the glory and honor and praise.

I pray today for my special friend and partner.

*Awaken Uncommon Faith* like an Explosion of Blessing...waves of understanding...sweeping across their life. Unlock the Windows of Heaven and unleash a financial river and anointing upon them...unlike anything they have ever experienced.

Whatever Faith Level they choose for their focus...honor it significantly...swiftly...undeniably.

Precious Father, give my partner today a revelation of this...that will bring provision for their own family...their personal business...their own ministry...for the rest of their lives.

I ask You for this in the Name of Jesus, who gave His life for us. Amen."

# ❧ 13 ❧

# 31 Days To Achieving Your Uncommon Dream

1. Your Uncommon Dream Is Anything You Want To *Become*, *Do* Or *Have* During Your Lifetime.
2. Your Uncommon Dream Must Be *Believed*, *Pursued* And *Protected* To Be Achieved.
3. Your Uncommon Dream Can Come True Regardless Of Your Personal Limitations.
4. Your Uncommon Dream Should Always Determine What You Do *First* Each Morning.
5. The Uncommon Dream You Are Pursuing Will Always Control And Dictate Your Daily Conduct And Behavior.
6. Your Daily Conversation Is A Portrait Of Your Passion For The Uncommon Dream You Are Pursuing.
7. Every Daily *Appointment* Should Be A Stepping Stone Toward The Fulfillment Of Your Uncommon Dream.
8. Your Uncommon Dream May Birth Changes In Your Relationships.
9. Your Uncommon Dream Will Determine Who Reaches For You.
10. Your Uncommon Dream Should Be Born Within You, Not Borrowed From Others.
11. Your Uncommon Dream May Require A Geographical Change.
12. Your Uncommon Dream Determines Who Qualifies For Access.
13. Your Uncommon Dream Should Qualify For Your Total Focus.
14. Your Uncommon Dream Will Require Seasons Of Preparation.
15. Achieving Your Uncommon Dream May Require An Uncommon Mentor.
16. Your Uncommon Dream Is Your True Significant Difference From Another.
17. Satan Will Often Use Memories Of Your Past Failures To Distort The Uncommon Dream God Is Developing In You.
18. Your Success Cannot Begin Until You Fuel Your Passion For The Uncommon Dream Within You.
19. Your Family May Often Focus On Your Weaknesses Instead Of The Uncommon Dream Growing Within You.
20. If You Neglect The Uncommon Dream Within You, It Will Eventually Wither And Die.
21. Your Uncommon Dream May Require Uncommon Faith.
22. Your Uncommon Dream May Be Birthed From Uncommon Tragedies And Painful Memories.
23. Your Uncommon Dream May Be Misunderstood By Those Closest To You.
24. Your Uncommon Dream May Be So Great That It Makes You Feel Fearful, Inadequate Or Inferior.
25. Your Uncommon Dream Is Your Invisible Companion Accompanying You From Your Present Into Your Future.
26. The Passion For Your Uncommon Dream Must Increase So Strong That It Burns Within You Without The Encouragement Of Others.
27. Your Uncommon Dream May Expose Adversarial Relationships In Your Life.
28. Your Uncommon Dream Will Require Uncommon Favor From Others.
29. Every Relationship Will Move You Toward Your Uncommon Dream Or Away From It.
30. When You Boldly Announce Your Uncommon Dream, You Will Create An Instant Bond With Every Person Who Wants To Accomplish The Same Dream.
31. You Must Practice Continual Visualization Of Your Uncommon Dream.

| Topic | Thought |
|-------|---------|
|       |         |

# 14
# THE COVENANT OF 58 BLESSINGS

1. **Abilities** - Ex. 31:3; Rom. 12:6; 1 Cor. 12:4-7
2. **Abundance** - Dt. 15:6-7; 30:9; Ps. 92:12
3. **Angels** - Ps. 34:7; 91:11-12; Is. 63:9
4. **Assurance** - Gen. 26:3; Ezk. 34:16; Jn. 14:18
5. **Authority** - Gen. 1:27-28; 9:2; 2 Sam. 2:30
6. **Church** - Ps. 122:1; Is. 54:17; Hag. 2:9; Rom. 12:5
7. **Confidence** - Is. 40:31; 2 Cor. 3:5; 9:8
8. **Deliverance** - Ex. 3:8; 2 Ki. 17:39; Ps. 18:19
9. **Eternal Life** - Job 19:25-26; Matt. 16:25,27
10. **Eternal Honor** - Mal. 3:17; James 1:12; 1 Pet. 1:4
11. **Faith** - Lk. 17:6; Rom. 1:17; 5:1-2
12. **Faithfulness Of God** - Num. 23:19; 1 Ki. 8:56
13. **Family** - Gen. 15:4-5; 22:17-18; 28:14
14. **Favor** - Gen. 12:2; Ps. 5:12; 30:5,7; Pro. 3:4
15. **Fellowship With God** - Dt. 31:8; Pro. 1:33
16. **Forgiveness** - Ps. 130:3-4; Is. 43:25; Matt. 6:14
17. **Freedom From Fear** - Ps. 46:1-2; 56:3-4,9
18. **Freedom From Worry** - Ps. 3:5-6; 55:12
19. **Friendship** - Pro. 17:17; 18:24; 27:10
20. **Fruitfulness** - Dt. 28:4; Ps. 1:3; 92:14
21. **Grace** - Ps. 103:12-14; Is. 53:5; Rom. 5:20
22. **Guidance** - Ps. 25:9; 32:8; 73:23-25
23. **Happiness** - Ps. 37:4-5; 63:4-5; 64:10
24. **Health** - Ex. 15:26; Ps. 103:2-3; 147:3; Jer. 30:17
25. **Heaven** - Dan. 12:3; Mk. 14:25; Jn. 14:2
26. **Holy Spirit** - Lk. 11:13; Jn. 7:38; 14:26
27. **Hope** - Ps. 71:5; 119:49,81; Rom. 5:4-5
28. **Inspiration** - Job 32:8; Ps. 119:92,105; Pro. 20:27
29. **Intercession** - Is. 53:12; Mk. 11:24; Lk. 18:1
30. **Joy** - Neh. 8:10; Ps. 3:3; 16:11; 30:5
31. **Justice** - Job 8:3; 37:23; Ps. 72:4; 89:14
32. **Knowledge** - 2 Chr. 1:12; Job 36:4; Ps. 94:10
33. **Longevity** - Dt. 4:40; 11:21; Ps. 21:4
34. **Love** - Jn. 3:16; 15:10,12; Rom. 5:8
35. **Marriage** - Gen. 2:24; Ps. 128:3; Pro. 18:22
36. **Mercy** - Gen. 9:16; 39:21; Ex. 33:19
37. **Miracles** - Ex. 14:27-30; Ps. 105:39-40; Matt. 19:26
38. **Ministry** - Is. 61:1; Matt. 22:14; Jn. 15:16
39. **Peace** - Lev. 26:6; Ps. 29:11; 72:7; Is. 26:3
40. **Power** - Ex. 9:16; Dt. 4:37; 11:25; Is. 59:19
41. **Promotion** - Dt. 28:13; 1 Sam. 2:8; Ps. 71:21
42. **Prosperity** - Gen. 13:14-15; Lev. 20:24; 26:9
43. **Protection** - Dt. 1:30; 2 Chr. 20:15; Ps. 91:2-7
44. **Provision** - Dt. 8:7-9; 28:3,5; 1 Ki. 17:14
45. **Rest** - Ps. 4:8; 23:2; Pro. 1:33; 3:24
46. **Restoration** - Job 42:10; Ps. 23:3; 40:2-3
47. **Resurrection** - Is. 25:8; Jn. 5:21; 11:25-26
48. **Riches** - Dt. 8:18; 1 Chr. 29:12; Pro. 8:18-19
49. **Salvation** - Ps. 27:1; 55:16; Jn. 6:54; Rom. 1:16
50. **Security** - Ps. 26:1; 57:3; 62:2,7; 105:14-15
51. **Strength** - Josh. 23:9; 1 Chr. 16:27; Ps. 18:2,29,32
52. **Success** - Josh. 1:5,7-8; Ps. 112:1-2; Is. 58:11
53. **Truth** - Num.23:19; Ps. 91:4b; Mk. 4:22
54. **Understanding** - 1 Ki. 3:12; Ps. 111:10; 119:130
55. **Victory** - Ps. 60:12; 108:13; 1 Cor. 15:55-57
56. **Wisdom** - 1 Ki. 4:29; Pro. 2:6-7; Lk. 21:15
57. **Word Of God** - Ps. 1:2; 19:7-8; 107:20
58. **Work** - Ex. 23:12; Dt. 15:10; 28:2,12; Ps.1:3

# MY 12 MONTH SEED GOALS

| Month | Seed Focus | Fulfillment Date |
|---|---|---|
| January | | |
| February | | |
| March | | |
| April | | |
| May | | |
| June | | |
| July | | |
| August | | |
| September | | |
| October | | |
| November | | |
| December | | |

## Yes, Mike, I Have A Special Prayer Request...

PLEASE REMOVE THIS PORTION AND RETURN IT IN THE ENCLOSED ENVELOPE.

The Wisdom Center • 4051 Denton Highway • Fort Worth, TX 76117 • Ph: (817) 759-0300 • www.TheWisdomCenter.tv

*Please agree with me in prayer for the following:*

_____

_____

_____

_____

_____

_____

_____

_____

_____

_____

*Name*

NBPR

# JOIN THE
# Wisdom Key 3000 TODAY!

Dear Partner,

*God has connected us!*

I have asked The Holy Spirit for 3000 Special Partners who will plant a monthly Seed of $58.00 to help me bring the gospel around the world. (58 represents 58 kinds of blessings in the Bible.)

Will you become my monthly Faith Partner in The Wisdom Key 3000? Your monthly Seed of $58.00 is so powerful in helping heal broken lives. When you sow into the work of God, 4 Miracle Harvests are guaranteed in Scripture, Isaiah 58...

► Uncommon Health (Isaiah 58)
► Uncommon Wisdom For Decision-Making (Isaiah 58)
► Uncommon Financial Favor (Isaiah 58)
► Uncommon Family Restoration (Isaiah 58)

Your Faith Partner,

*Mike Murdock*

PP-03

---

| Topic | Thought |
|-------|---------|
|       |         |

# 17

# ONE YEAR BIBLE READING SCHEDULE

**JANUARY**
1. Gen. 1-3
2. Gen. 4-6
3. Gen. 7-9
4. Gen. 10-14
5. Gen. 15-17
6. Gen. 18-20
7. Gen. 21-23
8. Gen. 24-26
9. Gen. 27-29
10. Gen. 30-32
11. Gen. 33-37
12. Gen. 38-40
13. Gen. 41-43
14. Gen. 44-46
15. Gen. 47-49
16. Gen. 50-Ex. 2
17. Ex. 3-5
18. Ex. 6-10
19. Ex. 11-13
20. Ex. 14-16
21. Ex. 17-19
22. Ex. 20-22
23. Ex. 23-25
24. Ex. 26-28
25. Ex. 29-33
26. Ex. 34-36
27. Ex. 37-39
28. Ex. 40-Lev. 2
29. Lev. 3-5
30. Lev. 6-8
31. Lev. 9-11

**FEBRUARY**
1. Lev. 12-16
2. Lev. 17-19
3. Lev. 20-22
4. Lev. 23-25
5. Lev. 26-Num. 1
6. Num. 2-4
7. Num. 5-7
8. Num. 8-12
9. Num. 13-15
10. Num. 16-18
11. Num. 19-21
12. Num. 22-24
13. Num. 25-27
14. Num. 28-30
15. Num. 31-35
16. Num. 36-Deut. 2
17. Deut. 3-5
18. Deut. 6-8
19. Deut. 9-11
20. Deut. 12-14
21. Deut. 15-17
22. Deut. 18-22
23. Deut. 23-25
24. Deut. 26-28

**FEBRUARY** (continued)
25. Deut. 29-31
26. Deut. 32-34
27. Josh. 1-3
28. Josh. 4-6

**MARCH**
1. Josh. 7-11
2. Josh. 12-14
3. Josh. 15-17
4. Josh. 18-20
5. Josh. 21-23
6. Josh. 24-Judg. 2
7. Judg. 3-5
8. Judg. 6-10
9. Judg. 11-13
10. Judg. 14-16
11. Judg. 17-19
12. Judg. 21 Ruth 1
13. Ruth 2-4
14. 1 Sam. 1-3
15. 1 Sam. 4-8
16. 1 Sam. 9-11
17. 1 Sam. 12-14
18. 1 Sam. 15-17
19. 1 Sam. 18-20
20. 1 Sam. 21-23
21. 1 Sam. 24-26
22. 1 Sam. 27-31
23. 2 Sam. 1-3
24. 2 Sam. 4-6
25. 2 Sam. 7-9
26. 2 Sam. 10-12
27. 2 Sam. 13-15
28. 2 Sam. 16-18
29. 2 Sam. 19-23
30. 2 Sam.24-1 Ki. 2
31. 1 Ki. 3-5

**APRIL**
1. 1 Ki. 6-8
2. 1 Ki. 9-11
3. 1 Ki. 12-14
4. 1 Ki. 15-17
5. 1 Ki. 18-22
6. 2 Ki. 1-3
7. 2 Ki. 4-6
8. 2 Ki. 7-9
9. 2 Ki. 10-12
10. 2 Ki. 13-15
11. 2 Ki. 16-18
12. 2 Ki. 19-23
13. 2 Ki. 24-1 Chr. 1
14. 1 Chr. 2-4
15. 1 Chr. 5-7
16. 1 Chr. 8-10
17. 1 Chr. 11-13
18. 1 Chr. 14-16

**APRIL** (continued)
19. 1 Chr. 17-21
20. 1 Chr. 22-24
21. 1 Chr. 25-27
22. 1 Chr. 28-2 Chr. 1
23. 2 Chr. 2-4
24. 2 Chr. 5-7
25. 2 Chr. 8-10
26. 2 Chr. 11-15
27. 2 Chr. 16-18
28. 2 Chr. 19-21
29. 2 Chr. 22-24
30. 2 Chr. 25-27

**MAY**
1. 2 Chr. 28-30
2. 2 Chr. 31-33
3. 2 Chr. 34-Ez. 2
4. Ezra 3-5
5. Ezra 6-8
6. Ezra 9-Neh. 1
7. Neh. 2-4
8. Neh. 5-7
9. Neh. 8-10
10. Neh. 11-Esth. 2
11. Esth. 3-5
12. Esth. 6-8
13. Esth. 9-Job 1
14. Job 2-4
15. Job 5-7
16. Job 8-10
17. Job 11-15
18. Job 16-18
19. Job 19-21
20. Job 22-24
21. Job 25-27
22. Job 28-30
23. Job 31-33
24. Job 34-38
25. Job 39-41
26. Job 42-Ps. 2
27. Ps. 3-5
28. Ps. 6-8
29. Ps. 9-11
30. Ps. 12-14
31. Ps. 15-19

**JUNE**
1. Ps. 20-22
2. Ps. 23-25
3. Ps. 26-28
4. Ps. 29-31
5. Ps. 32-34
6. Ps. 35-37
7. Ps. 38-42
8. Ps. 43-45
9. Ps. 46-48
10. Ps. 49-51
11. Ps. 52-54
12. Ps. 55-57

**JUNE** (continued)
13. Ps. 58-60
14. Ps. 61-65
15. Ps. 66-68
16. Ps. 69-71
17. Ps. 72-74
18. Ps. 75-77
19. Ps. 78-80
20. Ps. 81-83
21. Ps. 84-88
22. Ps. 89-91
23. Ps. 92-94
24. Ps. 95-97
25. Ps. 98-100
26. Ps. 101-103
27. Ps. 104-106
28. Ps. 107-111
29. Ps. 112-114
30. Ps. 115-117

**JULY**
1. Ps. 118-120
2. Ps. 121-123
3. Ps. 124-126
4. Ps. 127-129
5. Ps. 130-134
6. Ps. 135-137
7. Ps. 138-140
8. Ps. 141-143
9. Ps. 144-146
10. Ps. 147-149
11. Ps. 150-Prov. 2
12. Prov. 3-7
13. Prov. 8-10
14. Prov. 11-13
15. Prov. 14-16
16. Prov. 17-19
17. Prov. 20-22
18. Prov. 23-25
19. Prov. 26-30
20. Prov. 31-Ecc. 2
21. Eccl. 3-5
22. Eccl. 6-8
23. Eccl. 9-11
24. Eccl.12-Song 2
25. Song 3-5
26. Song 6-Isa. 2
27. Isa. 3-5
28. Isa. 6-8
29. Isa. 9-11
30. Isa. 12-14
31. Isa. 15-17

**AUGUST**
1. Isa. 18-20
2. Isa. 21-25
3. Isa. 26-28
4. Isa. 29-31
5. Isa. 32-34
6. Isa. 35-37

**AUGUST** (continued)
7. Isa. 38-40
8. Isa. 41-43
9. Isa. 44-48
10. Isa. 49-51
11. Isa. 52-54
12. Isa. 55-57
13. Isa. 58-60
14. Isa. 61-63
15. Isa. 64-66
16. Jer. 1-5
17. Jer. 6-8
18. Jer. 9-11
19. Jer. 12-14
20. Jer. 15-17
21. Jer. 18-20
22. Jer. 21-23
23. Jer. 24-28
24. Jer. 29-31
25. Jer. 32-34
26. Jer. 35-37
27. Jer. 38-40
28. Jer. 41-43
29. Jer. 44-46
30. Jer. 47-51
31. Jer. 52-Lam. 2

**SEPTEMBER**
1. Lam. 3-5
2. Ezek. 1-3
3. Ezek. 4-6
4. Ezek. 7-9
5. Ezek. 10-12
6. Ezek. 13-17
7. Ezek. 18-20
8. Ezek. 21-23
9. Ezek. 24-26
10. Ezek. 27-29
11. Ezek. 30-32
12. Ezek. 33-35
13. Ezek. 36-40
14. Ezek. 41-43
15. Ezek. 44-46
16. Ezek. 47-Dan. 1
17. Dan. 2-4
18. Dan. 5-7
19. Dan. 8-10
20. Dan 11-Hos. 3
21. Hos. 4-6
22. Hos. 7-9
23. Hos. 10-12
24. Hos. 13-Joel 1
25. Joel 2-Amos 1
26. Amos 2-4
27. Amos 5-9
28. Obad. 1-Jonah 2
29. Jonah 3-Mic. 1
30. Mic. 2-4

**OCTOBER**
1. Mic. 5-7

**OCTOBER** (continued)

2. Nah. 1-3
3. Hab. 1-3
4. Zeph. 1-Hag. 2
5. Zech. 1-3
6. Zech. 4-6
7. Zech. 7-9
8. Zech. 10-12
9. Zech. 13-14
10. Mal. 1-4
11. Matt. 1-5
12. Matt. 6-8
13. Matt. 9-11
14. Matt. 12-14
15. Matt. 15-17
16. Matt. 18-20
17. Matt. 21-23
18. Matt. 24-28
19. Mk. 1-3
20. Mk. 4-6
21. Mk. 7-9
22. Mk. 10-12
23. Mk. 13-15
24. Mk. 16-Lk. 2
25. Lk. 3-7
26. Lk. 8-10
27. Lk. 11-13
28. Lk. 14-16
29. Lk. 17-19
30. Lk. 20-22
31. Lk. 23-Jn. 1

**NOVEMBER**

1. Jn. 2-6
2. Jn. 7-9
3. Jn. 10-12
4. Jn. 13-15
5. Jn. 16-18
6. Jn. 19-21
7. Acts 1-3
8. Acts 4-8
9. Acts 9-11
10. Acts 12-14
11. Acts 15-17
12. Acts 18-20
13. Acts 21-23
14. Acts 24-26
15. Acts 27-Rom. 3
16. Rom. 4-6
17. Rom. 7-9
18. Rom. 10-12
19. Rom. 13-15
20. Rom. 16-1 Cor. 2
21. 1 Cor. 3-5
22. 1 Cor. 6-10
23. 1 Cor. 11-13
24. 1 Cor. 14-16
25. 2 Cor. 1-3
26. 2 Cor. 4-6
27. 2 Cor. 7-9
28. 2 Cor. 10-12
29. 2 Cor. 13-Gal. 4
30. Gal. 5-Eph. 1

**DECEMBER**

1. Eph. 2-4
2. Eph. 5-Phil. 1
3. Phil. 2-4
4. Col. 1-3
5. Col. 4-1 Thess. 2
6. 1 Thess. 3-2 Thess. 2
7. 2 Thess. 3-1 Tim. 2
8. 1 Tim. 3-5
9. 1 Tim. 6-2 Tim. 2
10. 2 Tim. 3-Titus 1
11. Titus 2-Philem. 1
12. Heb. 1-3
13. Heb. 4-8
14. Heb. 9-11
15. Heb. 12-James 1
16. James 2-4
17. James 5-1 Pet. 2
18. 1 Pet. 3-5
19. 2 Pet. 1-3
20. 1 Jn. 1-5
21. 2 Jn. 1-Jude 1
22. Rev. 1-3
23. Rev. 4-5
24. Rev. 6-7
25. Rev. 8-9
26. Rev. 10-11
27. Rev. 12-16
28. Rev. 17-18
29. Rev. 19-20
30. Rev. 21-22
31. Well Done!

# ☙ 18 ☙
## READING THE BIBLE THROUGH IN ONE MONTH

1. Gen. 1-40
2. Gen. 41 / Ex. 1-30
3. Ex. 31-40 / Lev. 1-27 / Num. 1-3
4. Num. 4-36 / Deut. 1-7
5. Deut. 8-34 / Josh. 1-13
6. Josh. 14-24 / Judg. 1-21 / Ruth 1-4 / 1 Sam. 1-4
7. 1 Sam. 5-31 / 2 Sam. 1-13
8. 2 Sam. 14-24 / 1 Ki. 1-22 / 2 Ki. 1-7
9. 2 Ki. 8-25 / 1 Chr. 1-22
10. 1 Chr. 23-29 / 2 Chr. 1-33
11. 2 Chr. 34-36 / Ezra 1-10 / Neh. 1-13 / Esth. 1-10 / Job 1-4
12. Job 5-42 / Ps. 1-2
13. Ps. 3-42
14. Ps. 43-82
15. Ps. 83-122
16. Ps. 123-150 / Prov. 1-12
17. Prov. 13-31 / Eccl. 1-12 / Song 1-8 / Isa. 1
18. Isa. 2-41
19. Isa. 42-66 / Jer. 1-15
20. Jer. 16-52 / Lam. 1-3
21. Lam. 4-5 / Ezek. 1-40
22. Ezek. 41-48 / Dan. 1-12 / Hos. 1-14 / Joel 1-3 / Amos 1-3
23. Amos 4-9 / Obad. 1 / Jonah 1-4 / Mic. 1-7 / Nah. 1-3 / Hab. 1-3 / Zeph. 1-3 / Hag. 1-2 / Zech. 1-14 / Mal. 1-4
24. Matt. 1-28 / Mk. 1-12
25. Mk. 13-16 / Lk. 1-24 / Jn. 1-12
26. Jn. 13-21 / Acts 1-28 / Rom. 1-3
27. Rom. 4-16 / 1 Cor. 1-16 / 2 Cor. 1-11
28. 2 Cor. 12-13 / Gal. 1-6 / Eph. 1-6 / Phil. 1-4 / Col. 1-4 / 1 Thess. 1-5 / 2 Thess. 1-3 / 1 Tim. 1-6 / 2 Tim. 1-4
29. Titus 1-3 / Philem. 1 / Heb. 1-13 / James 1-5 / 1 Pet. 1-5 / 2 Pet. 1-3 / 1 Jn. 1-5 / 2 Jn. 1 / 3 Jn. 1 / Jude 1
30. Rev. 1-22

# TAX PLANNING TIPS...

- **Charitable gifts** are generally deductible in amounts up to 50% of adjusted gross income (AGI) for gifts of cash and 30% of AGI for gifts of appreciated property.

- **When appreciated securities are donated...** you are entitled to a deduction for full value, not just the original cost. This results in a tax deduction based on "paper profits" you have not yet realized. If securities have decreased in value, consider selling them, thereby creating a loss for tax purposes, and making deductible gifts of the cash proceeds.

- **Consider making larger gifts** in years when you have more income and will be in a higher tax bracket. The higher your tax bracket, the greater the savings from your gifts.

**The Legacy Program**

**THE WISDOM CENTER**

ning For
uture!

Dear Partner,

**YOUR SEED MAKES A DIFFERENCE.**

You have made it possible for thousands to hear the Gospel around the world through the multi-faceted outreaches of **The Wisdom Center...** Thank you!

In addition to saying thank you, we would like to share information with you on how your generosity can have an ongoing effect now, and, in the years to come. Take a few minutes and review this crucial information about how you can receive the maximum benefit from your Financial Gifts (Seeds) to this Ministry.

It is your Faithful Gifts and Seed that make it possible for us to Pursue... Proclaim... and Publish the Wisdom of God throughout the world.

Your Faith Partner,

Mike Murdock

Dr. Mike Murdock
Founder, Senior Pastor
The Wisdom Center

## ASK YOURSELF THESE FOUR QUESTIONS!

1 **Did you receive and save your gift receipt?** It is especially important to keep your receipts for gifts of $250 or more and file them with your tax records. These receipts must state that you did not receive any benefits in return for your gift that have not been accounted for in the amount stated on the receipt.

2 **Are you enjoying maximum tax savings?** Cash gifts may be deductible from your federal income tax return. Many states also allow income tax deductions for charitable gifts. Charitable gifts included in your estate plans can result in significant tax savings as well.

3 **Does your employer match your charitable gifts?** If so, each gift you make is effectively doubled. Please check with your employer about this possibility.

4 **Have you reviewed your long-range financial and estate plans recently?** Tax & Estate Laws can change making this an essential step to planning effectively.

Your will, living trust, retirement plans, and other gifts and estate planning vehicles can provide another opportunity to support your favorite charitable interests.

## FINANCES FOR YOUR FUTURE

Everyone wants to know that their life is making a difference, both now and in the future. The ideas below are examples of how your generosity (Seed) can continue to make a difference today, and, in the years to come.

1 **A gift included in your will or living trust** is one way to establish a lasting legacy.

2 **A gift of retirement assets, such as pension plans or Individual Retirement Accounts** (IRAs), may allow you to give more than you thought possible, while eliminating taxes that may otherwise largely consume these assets.

3 **Consider gifts of life insurance.** Gifts of policies or proceeds you may no longer need offer excellent tax benefits. Life insurance can also be used to "replace" assets given away, thereby providing for loved ones in addition to your charitable interests.

4 **A life income gift can be a tax-effective** way to provide you and/or someone you designate with regular payments for life.

*Gifts in any of these forms can be made in memory or in honor of special loved ones. Complete and return the form on the reverse side for more information on these and other options you may want to consider.*

# The Legacy Program
## THE WISDOM CENTER

## The Legacy Program At The Wisdom Center

✓ Please send me more information on Gift and Estate Planning Ideas that will help me maximize my Financial Gifts (Seeds)...for the furtherance of the Gospel.

Name _____

Address _____

City _____ State _____ Zip _____

Phone _____ Email _____

☐ I have already included **The Wisdom Center** in my will and long term planning.

☐ I will consider including **The Wisdom Center** in my will and long term planning.

☐ Please have The Legacy Program Director contact me for further information.

NBLGY

*Mail to:*
**The Wisdom Center / Legacy Program**
4051 Denton Highway • Fort Worth, TX 76117-2042
OFFICE: 1-817-759-0300  FAX: 1-817-759-0310
**THEWISDOMCENTER.TV**

43

# A TREASURY of WISDOM

## The Master Secret Of Life Is Wisdom.

▶ Wisdom Determines Your Joy.

▶ Wisdom Determines Your Favor.

▶ Wisdom Determines Your Health.

▶ Wisdom Determines Your Success.

▶ Wisdom Determines Your Wealth.

▶ Wisdom Is The Golden Gate To Greatness.

▶ Wisdom Is The Mysterious Magnet For Miracles.

▶ Wisdom Is The Unseen Persuader For Effective Negotiation.

▶ Wisdom Is The Unstoppable Weapon Of Every Winning Warrior.

▶ Wisdom Is The Master Secret For Every Successful Marriage.

▶ Wisdom Is The Ability To Solve A Problem.

▶ Wisdom Is Simply The Law Of God... Applied Accurately To Solve A Problem.

▶ Wisdom Is The Scriptural Solution To Any Problem You Are Experiencing.

▶ Ignorance Is The Only True Enemy Capable Of Destroying You.

*–DR. MIKE MURDOCK*

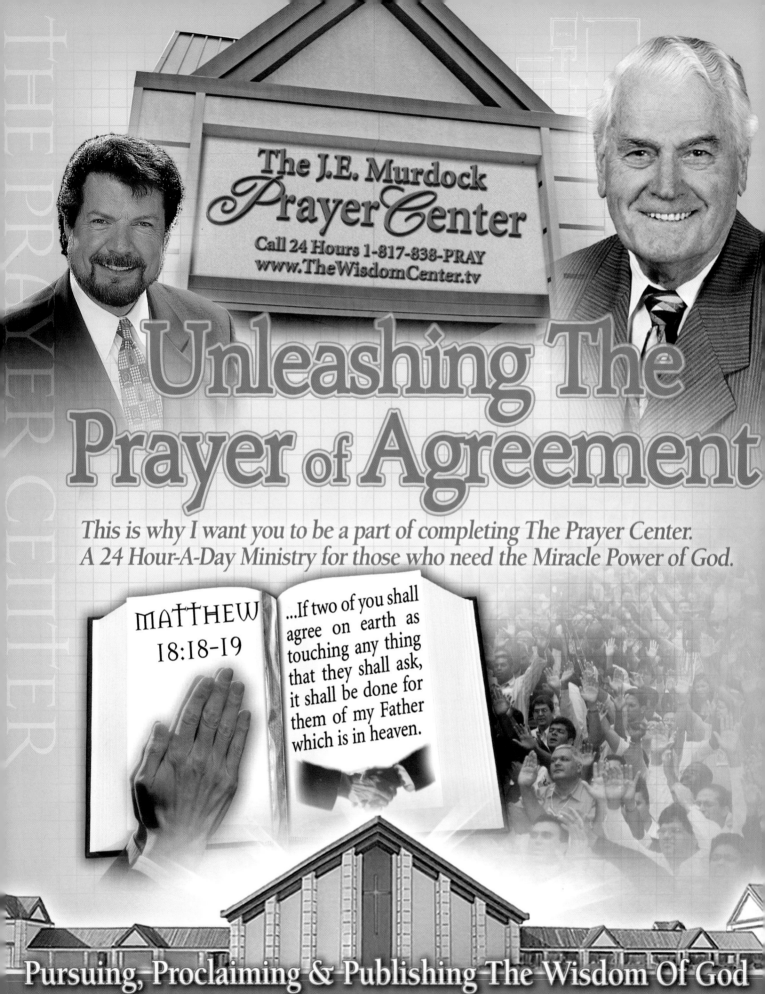

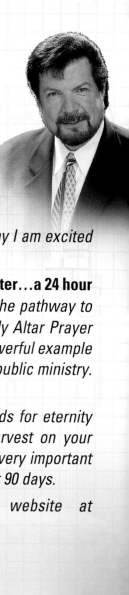

## My Precious Partner,

*These are crisis times.*

**Terrorism has paralyzed millions with fear.**

*People are calling the psychic hotlines in a frenzy… to know the future... to find some hope… some peace of mind… some escape from their anxiety. Suicide hotlines are busier than ever. Mental disorders are at an all time high. People are desperate for answers…and hungry for the supernatural… even recent movies reveal this.*

*You and I can have an Assignment to unleash the healing Wisdom of God. That is why I am excited about our new focus:* **The Prayer Center.**

**Champions know the power of prayer!** *That is why we are completing* **The Prayer Center…a 24 hour answer for the hurting…** *Communication with God is the only pathway to true peace…the pathway to daily strength. Prayer effects destiny. My father's life has proven this. We had a Family Altar Prayer twice a day… every morning and night... the 18 years I was at home... that was my most powerful example of prayer. In 1954, Daddy decided he could accomplish more by praying than he could in public ministry. I believe that everything we did was giving birth to The Secret Place...in prayer.*

*Our present estimate to complete The Prayer Center is only $120,000. The dividends for eternity cannot be measured. The opportunity… to make a difference and experience a Harvest on your investment…is powerful and unique. This is why I am inviting you to participate in this very important project. I have asked God for 120 of our friends and partners…to sow a $1,000 in the next 90 days.*

*Remember to register today for our upcoming conference on our website at* **www.TheWisdomCenter.tv.** *Looking forward to seeing you soon.*

*Your Faithful Prayer Partner,*

*Mike Murdock*

**PS. In celebrating Your Seed of $1,000 or more your name will be engraved on a beautiful Gold Plaque inside The Prayer Center.** *When you write explain that your Seed is for The Prayer Center in the memo section of your check. (Please write the name you want on the plaque very clearly. Your Seed can be in memory or honor of someone important to you.)*

**PPS. My extra Gift of Appreciation for any Seed of $100 or more is The Mike Murdock Wisdom Library, The Leadership Secrets of Jesus (Volume 4).** *Please remember to request this Gift of Appreciation when you write to me.*

# MY GIFT OF APPRECIATION...
## For My Special Friends And Partners!

# THE Wisdom Library OF Mike Murdock©

## VOLUME 4 IS NOW READY FOR YOUR LIBRARY!

**Every Home Should Contain A Library Of Wisdom. An Unforgettable Gift To Those You Love!**

This Beautiful Hardback Leatherette Collectors Edition combines two full-sized books contained in one volume.

► *The Leadership Secrets Of Jesus*
► *The Jesus Book*

**VOLUME 4 IS MY SPECIAL GIFT OF APPRECIATION THIS MONTH TO MY SPECIAL FRIENDS AND PARTNERS...**

*My prayer to God to give me special friends and partners is being answered. The completion of The Prayer Center is costly but will unleash the Prayer of Agreement and be powerful in healing the broken. Your faithful sowing to help sponsor this ministry is an answer to prayer, too. Expect your Uncommon Seed to create an Uncommon Harvest as you plant your Seed towards The Prayer Center today. I wanted to create a unique and invaluable Celebration of your Seed by presenting Volume 4 of The Wisdom Library...just for you!*

## WHEN YOU GET INVOLVED WITH GOD'S DREAM...HE WILL GET INVOLVED WITH YOURS!

MY GIFT OF APPRECIATION
**GIFT OF APPRECIATION**
Wisdom Is The Principal Thing

THE Mike Murdock COLLECTOR'S EDITION

Leadership Secrets Of Jesus
The Jesus Book
WISDOM KEY 3000 PARTNER EDITION

The Wisdom Center • 4051 Denton Highway • Fort Worth, TX 76117 • Ph: (817) 759-0300 • www.TheWisdomCenter.tv

---

# Yes, Mike, I Believe In The Power Of Prayer!
PLEASE REMOVE THIS PORTION AND RETURN IT IN THE ENCLOSED ENVELOPE.

NBPC1 ☐ Enclosed is My **Special Prayer Seed** to complete The Prayer Center: ☐ $1,000 ☐ $500 ☐ $250 ☐ Other $_____

NBPC2 ☐ Within the next 90 Days I Will Send My **Special Seed** Of:
☐ $100 ☐ $58 ☐ Other $_____

NBPCGA ☐ Please Rush My Special Gift, **Volume 4 of The Mike Murdock Wisdom Library...The Leadership Secrets Of Jesus...B-199 (hardback edition).**

NAME _____

ADDRESS _____

CITY _____ STATE _____ ZIP CODE _____

PHONE _____ E-MAIL _____

## *My Gift of Appreciation To My Partners... An Unforgettable Gift To Those You Love!*

**Method of Payment** *(Your check may be electronically deposited.)*
☐ MONEY ORDER ☐ CHECK ☐ AMEX
☐ DISCOVER ☐ MASTER CARD ☐ VISA

CARD #_____-_____-_____-_____

EXP. DATE _____/_____ TOTAL ENCLOSED $_____

SIGNATURE _____
(SORRY NO C.O.D.'s)

**48**
NBPC

Your Seed Faith Offerings are used to support The Wisdom Center, and all its programs. Applicable law requires that we have the discretion to allocate donations in order to carry out our charitable purpose. In the event The Wisdom Center receives more funds for the project than needed, the excess will be used for another worthy outreach.

| Topic | Thought |
|---|---|
|  |  |

# THE WISDOM BIBLE

## Partnership Edition

### Over 120 Wisdom Study Guides Included Such As:

- ▶ *10 Qualities Of Uncommon Achievers*
- ▶ *18 Facts You Should Know About The Anointing*
- ▶ *21 Facts To Help You Identify Those Assigned To You*
- ▶ *31 Facts You Should Know About Your Assignment*
- ▶ *8 Keys That Unlock Victory In Every Attack*
- ▶ *22 Defense Techniques To Remember During Seasons Of Personal Attack*
- ▶ *20 Wisdom Keys And Techniques To Remember During An Uncommon Battle*
- ▶ *11 Benefits You Can Expect From God*
- ▶ *31 Facts You Should Know About Favor*
- ▶ *The Covenant Of 58 Blessings*
- ▶ *7 Keys To Receiving Your Miracle*
- ▶ *16 Facts You Should Remember About Contentious People*
- ▶ *5 Facts Solomon Taught About Contracts*
- ▶ *7 Facts You Should Know About Conflict*
- ▶ *6 Steps That Can Unlock Your Self-Confidence*
- ▶ *And Much More!*

**Your Partnership makes such a difference in The Wisdom Center Outreach Ministries.** I wanted to place a Gift in your hand that could last a **lifetime** for you and your family... **The Wisdom Study Bible.**

**40 Years of Personal Notes...**this Partnership Edition Bible contains 160 pages of my Personal Study Notes...that could forever change your Bible Study of The Word of God. This **Partnership Edition...**is my personal **Gift of Appreciation** when you sow your Sponsorship Seed of $1,000 to help us complete The Prayer Center and TV Studio Complex. An Uncommon Seed Always Creates An Uncommon Harvest!

**Thank you from my heart for your Seed of Obedience (Luke 6:38).**

*Mike*

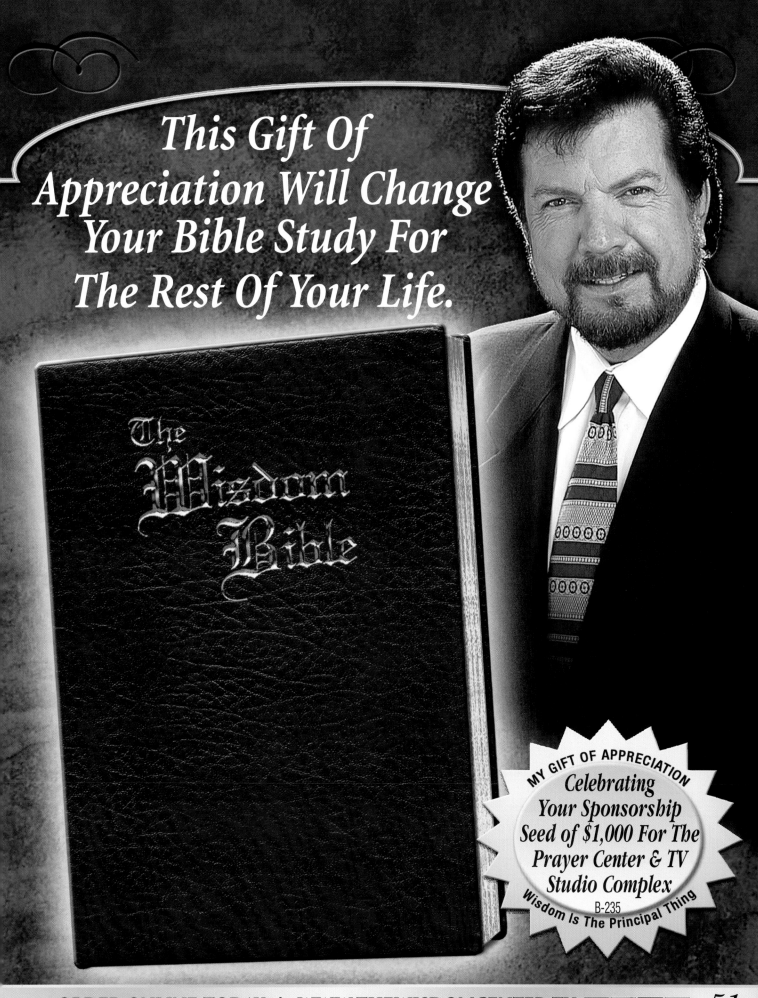

This Gift Of Appreciation Will Change Your Bible Study For The Rest Of Your Life.

The Wisdom Bible

# Wisdom Times

## *Wisdom Missions Tour Across The World...*

Sowing Wisdom In Puerto Rico...Brazil        Amsterdam...London...Congo...Africa...

We are seeing lives changed all across the world...! Your Seeds and Prayers HELP MAKE THIS HAPPEN.

"Go ye into all the world, and preach the gospel to every creature. And they went forth, and preached every where, the Lord working with them, and confirming the Word with signs following" (*Mark 16:15, 20*).

52

# Your Seed Is Making A Difference...!

I am asking every partner to sow generously this month for the spreading of the gospel. The wicked may be financing Terrorism, but God's people financing the gospel will receive their Harvests...Where they need it most! Jesus Guarantees it. *Mike*

**The Wisdom Center** • 4051 Denton Highway • Fort Worth, TX 76117 • Ph: (817) 759-0300 • www.TheWisdomCenter.tv

---

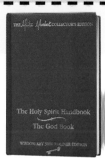

| Topic | Thought |
| --- | --- |
|  |  |

# HOME OF HOPE

**WOULD YOU HELP SPONSOR OUR BOYS' HOME IN SOUTH AFRICA?** THE MIKE MURDOCK HOME OF HOPE IS FOR CHILDREN WHOSE PARENTS HAVE BEEN VICTIMIZED BY AIDS.

I KNEW YOU WOULD WANT TO BE PART OF THIS!

**The Mike Murdock Home Of Hope**
Johannesburg
South Africa

Here are some pictures of our Dedication Day. Missionaries Michel and Natalie Chevalier flew to South Africa from their work in France to help celebrate the Dedication Day of Home Of Hope.

56

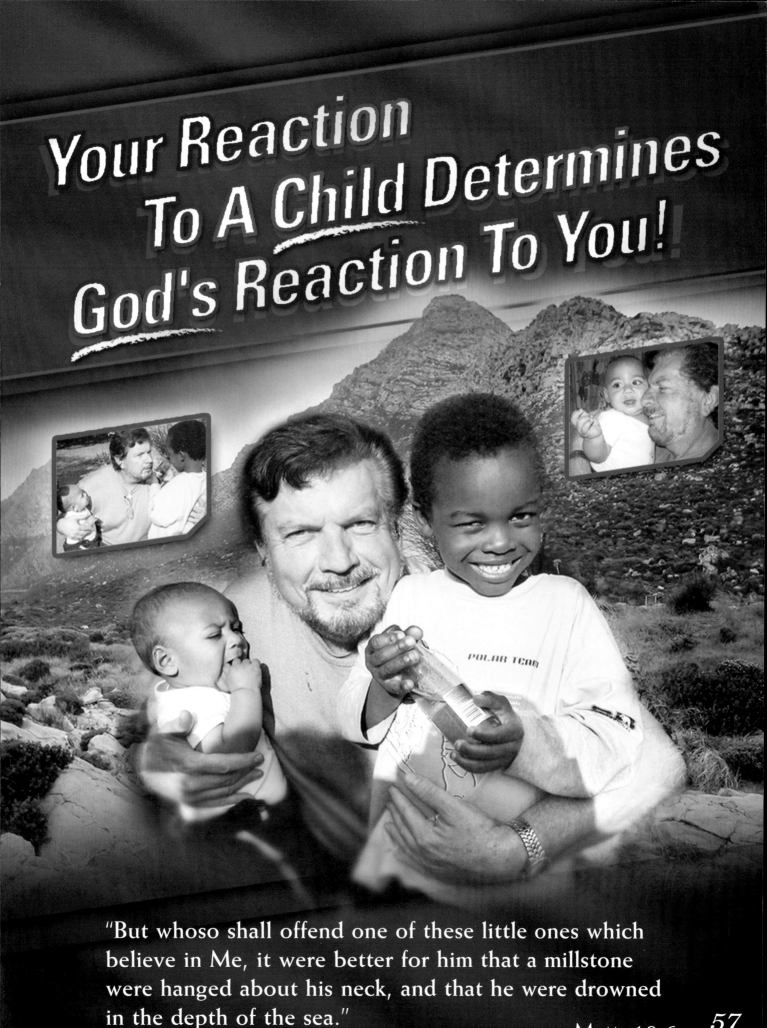

# Your Reaction To A Child Determines God's Reaction To You!

"But whoso shall offend one of these little ones which believe in Me, it were better for him that a millstone were hanged about his neck, and that he were drowned in the depth of the sea."

–Matt. 18:6

57

# MY GIFT OF APPRECIATION...

# The Wisdom Commentary 2!

## This Powerful Wisdom Book Is A Must For Every Family Library!

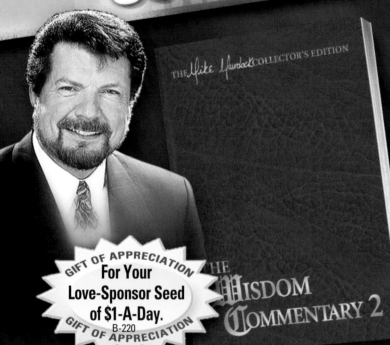

THE Mike Murdock COLLECTOR'S EDITION

THE WISDOM COMMENTARY 2

**GIFT OF APPRECIATION**
**For Your Love-Sponsor Seed of $1-A-Day.**
B-220
**GIFT OF APPRECIATION**

## MY GIFT OF APPRECIATION
*To My Love-Sponsors of Home of Hope...$1-A-Day.*

THIS PAPERBACK VOLUME OF THE WISDOM COMMENTARY 2 INCLUDES 52 DIFFERENT TOPICS...FOR MENTORING YOUR FAMILY EVERY WEEK OF THE YEAR.

*These topics include:*

| | | |
|---|---|---|
| ▸ Angels | ▸ Fathers | ▸ Overcoming |
| ▸ Anger | ▸ Fear | ▸ Passion |
| ▸ Appearance | ▸ Focus | ▸ Peace |
| ▸ Atmosphere | ▸ Forgetting | ▸ Planning |
| ▸ Attitude | ▸ The Past | ▸ Prayer Language |
| ▸ Church | ▸ Greatness | ▸ Relationships |
| ▸ Compassion | ▸ Habits | ▸ Respect |
| ▸ Conversation | ▸ Humility | ▸ Salvation |
| ▸ Crisis | ▸ Imagination | ▸ Servanthood |
| ▸ Delegation | ▸ Jealousy | ▸ Singing |
| ▸ Desire | ▸ Marriage | ▸ Spiritual Warfare |
| ▸ Disloyalty | ▸ Mothers | ▸ Submission |
| ▸ Distractions | ▸ Motivating | ▸ Talents And Skills |
| ▸ Expectation | Yourself | ▸ Tithing |
| ▸ Failure | ▸ Negotiation | ▸ Unthankfulness |
| ▸ Faith | ▸ Obedience | ▸ Voice of God |
| ▸ Faith-Talk | ▸ Opportunity | ▸ Vows |
| ▸ Fasting | ▸ Order | ▸ Waiting on God |

# The Wisdom Commentary 2!

- ▶ 41 Facts About Angels
- ▶ 17 Facts About Compassion
- ▶ 8 Facts You Should Remember In Every Conversation
- ▶ 9 Facts About Words You Should Remember
- ▶ 20 Important Facts To Remember During Crisis
- ▶ 9 Important Facts About Networking With Others
- ▶ 10 Facts About Disloyalty You Should Remember
- ▶ 3 Characteristics Of Disloyal People
- ▶ 6 Keys In Dealing With Disloyalty
- ▶ 13 Facts About A Successful Life
- ▶ 14 Wisdom Keys To Avoid Distractions And Protect Your Focus
- ▶ 14 Facts About The Law Of Expectation
- ▶ 9 Facts About Failure
- ▶ 4 Steps To Take After Times Of Failure
- ▶ 3 Things Satan Cannot Do
- ▶ 19 Facts About Faith
- ▶ 3 Ways To Increase Your Faith
- ▶ 30 Ways To Nurture Your Faith-Talk

- ▶ 3 Basic Reasons For Losing Your Motivation
- ▶ 26 Principles Of Successful Negotiation
- ▶ 18 Facts You Should Know About Obedience
- ▶ 8 Golden Opportunities You Must Recognize
- ▶ 30 Facts About Order
- ▶ 10 Facts Every Overcomer Must Remember
- ▶ 9 Facts About Your Passion
- ▶ 6 Facts About Peace
- ▶ 3 Ways The Holy Spirit Affects Your Peace
- ▶ 4 Keys To Creating A Peaceful Climate
- ▶ 11 Facts About Planning
- ▶ 15 Keys You Should Know About Tongues And Your Prayer Language
- ▶ 4 Kinds Of People Satan Will Use To Distract You, Demoralize You And Discourage You
- ▶ 4 Questions That Qualify People For Intimacy
- ▶ 8 Keys To Remember When A Relationship Is Ending
- ▶ 31 Keys In Protecting A Worthy Relationship
- ▶ 12 Things You Must Respect In Order To Succeed

MIKE MURDOCK HOME OF HOPE

- ▶ 27 Important Facts About Fasting
- ▶ 31 Qualities Of An Uncommon Father
- ▶ 14 Facts You Should Know About Fear
- ▶ 6 Keys That Will Help Protect Your Focus
- ▶ 20 Facts About The Weapon Of Forgetting
- ▶ 8 Facts You Should Remember About Greatness
- ▶ 13 Keys In Discerning Greatness In Others
- ▶ 12 Keys In Recognizing Personal Greatness
- ▶ 11 Facts About Your Habits
- ▶ 12 Daily Habits That Will Bring You To Uncommon Greatness
- ▶ 3 Proofs Of Humility
- ▶ 10 Facts About Humility
- ▶ 19 Facts About Imagination
- ▶ 7 Keys In Overcoming Envy And Jealousy
- ▶ 5 Things You Should Know About Your Mate
- ▶ 20 Success Keys To A Better Marriage
- ▶ 31 Qualities Of An Uncommon Mother
- ▶ 7 Keys To Motivating Yourself

- ▶ 31 Keys For New Believers
- ▶ 11 Facts About Servanthood
- ▶ 34 Facts About Singing
- ▶ Satan's 4 Favorite Weapons
- ▶ How To Predict Your 6 Seasons Of Satanic Attack
- ▶ Your 6 Most Effective Weapons In Battle
- ▶ 4 Forces That Shorten Your Season Of Struggle
- ▶ 31 Facts About Submission
- ▶ 9 Important Facts Concerning Your Gifts, Skills And Talents
- ▶ 17 Powerful Facts You Should Remember About Tithing
- ▶ 11 Facts About Thankfulness
- ▶ 14 Facts About Unthankfulness
- ▶ 8 Keys To Staying Thankful During Crisis
- ▶ 8 Rewards For Recognizing The Voice Of The Spirit
- ▶ 5 Facts About Vows
- ▶ 16 Rewards For Waiting On God
- ▶ 36 Facts About Waiting On God

THE WISDOM CENTER
4051 Denton Highway • Fort Worth, TX 76117
1-888-WISDOM-1
1-817-759-0300
Website:
TheWisdomCenter.tv

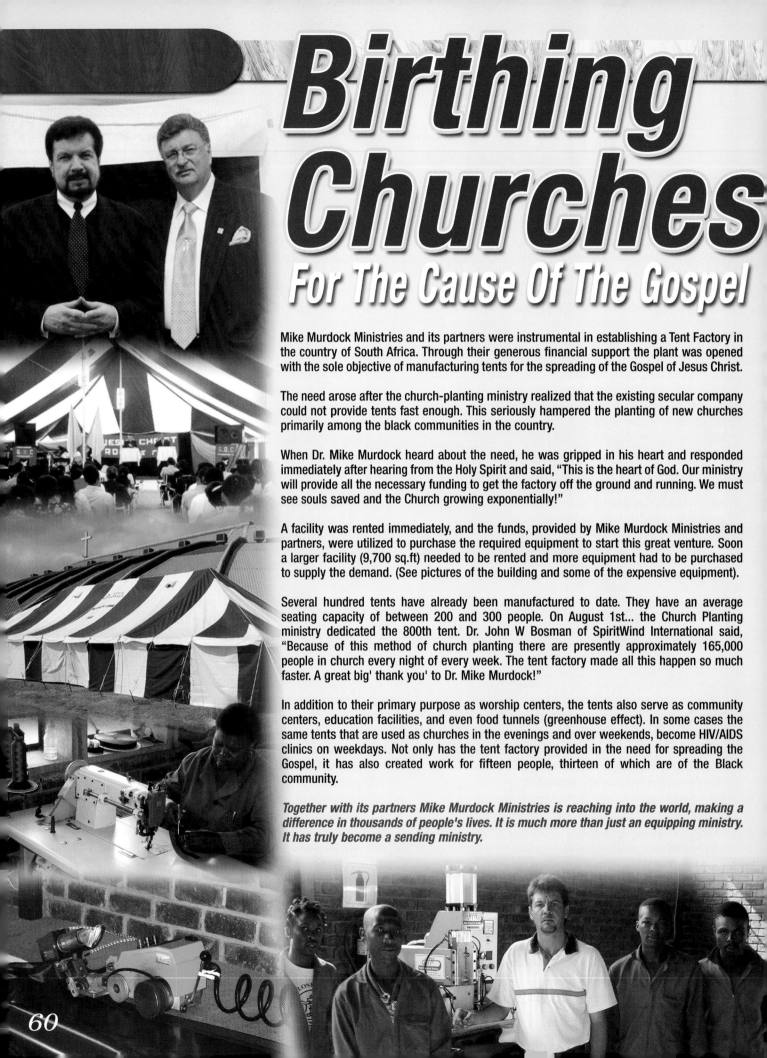

# Birthing Churches
## For The Cause Of The Gospel

Mike Murdock Ministries and its partners were instrumental in establishing a Tent Factory in the country of South Africa. Through their generous financial support the plant was opened with the sole objective of manufacturing tents for the spreading of the Gospel of Jesus Christ.

The need arose after the church-planting ministry realized that the existing secular company could not provide tents fast enough. This seriously hampered the planting of new churches primarily among the black communities in the country.

When Dr. Mike Murdock heard about the need, he was gripped in his heart and responded immediately after hearing from the Holy Spirit and said, "This is the heart of God. Our ministry will provide all the necessary funding to get the factory off the ground and running. We must see souls saved and the Church growing exponentially!"

A facility was rented immediately, and the funds, provided by Mike Murdock Ministries and partners, were utilized to purchase the required equipment to start this great venture. Soon a larger facility (9,700 sq.ft) needed to be rented and more equipment had to be purchased to supply the demand. (See pictures of the building and some of the expensive equipment).

Several hundred tents have already been manufactured to date. They have an average seating capacity of between 200 and 300 people. On August 1st... the Church Planting ministry dedicated the 800th tent. Dr. John W Bosman of SpiritWind International said, "Because of this method of church planting there are presently approximately 165,000 people in church every night of every week. The tent factory made all this happen so much faster. A great big' thank you' to Dr. Mike Murdock!"

In addition to their primary purpose as worship centers, the tents also serve as community centers, education facilities, and even food tunnels (greenhouse effect). In some cases the same tents that are used as churches in the evenings and over weekends, become HIV/AIDS clinics on weekdays. Not only has the tent factory provided in the need for spreading the Gospel, it has also created work for fifteen people, thirteen of which are of the Black community.

*Together with its partners Mike Murdock Ministries is reaching into the world, making a difference in thousands of people's lives. It is much more than just an equipping ministry. It has truly become a sending ministry.*

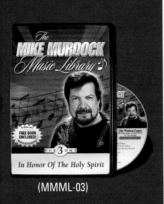

(MMML-03)

Ask for your
personal Gift
Music CD, *In Honor
Of The Holy Spirit*,
Volume 3, of the
Mike Murdock
Music Library...
powerful songs
ushering in the
Presence of God
all around the
world.

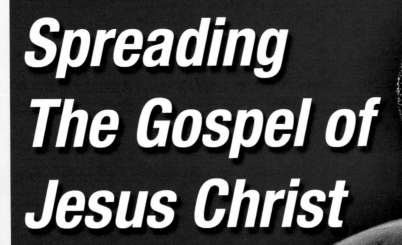

# Spreading The Gospel of Jesus Christ

Precious Partner,

Why do we travel around the world to South Africa, Nigeria, The Congo, Europe and Brazil?

We have a divine mandate. "Go ye into all the world, and preach the gospel" (Mark 16:15)

Your Seed is an investment that will have eternal dividends. *He that winneth souls is wise. (Proverbs 11:30)* **EXPECTANCY** of your Harvest...is vital! Remember to write and tell me about your Special Harvest, too.

Expecting An Uncommon Harvest,

Mike

The Wisdom Center • 4051 Denton Highway • Fort Worth, TX • Ph: (817) 759-0300 • www.TheWisdomCenter.tv

---

## Yes, Mike I Want To Make A Difference In Africa...And Around The World...!

PLEASE REMOVE THIS PORTION AND RETURN IT IN THE ENCLOSED ENVELOPE.

NBAW1 ☐ Enclosed is My **Special Seed of $**_____ to help you minister the gospel around the world.

NBAW2 ☐ Enclosed is My **Wisdom Key 3000** Monthly Faith Promise of $58 to help you spread the Gospel.

BAWGA ☐ Please Rush My Gift Music CD...*In Honor Of The Holy Spirit.*
    (This is Volume 3 of the new Collector's Edition of The Mike Murdock Music Library!) (MMML-03)

(MMML-03)

NAME _____

ADDRESS _____

CITY _____ STATE _____ ZIP CODE _____

PHONE _____ E-MAIL _____

**Method of Payment** *(Your check may be electronically deposited.)*
☐ MONEY ORDER  ☐ CHECK  ☐ AMEX
☐ DISCOVER  ☐ MASTER CARD  ☐ VISA

CARD #_____-_____-_____-_____

EXP. DATE ____/____    TOTAL ENCLOSED $_____

SIGNATURE _____
(SORRY NO C.O.D.'s)

61

# Wisdom for Asia

**This Is Our Season of Opportunity!**

The Wisdom Center is proclaiming the Wisdom of God in India. God has divinely connected us there to a great man of God, Pastor T. A. Thomas, Founder of Wisdom for Asia Ministries.

Pastor Thomas has been ministering there for over 33 years. He has given birth to over 75 churches and is constantly mentoring young ministers. For years, he carried out his ministry on foot, bicycle or over-crowded buses. We were so honored to provide him a new vehicle. To further accelerate his ministry, we have built a three-story Dormitory Building for Wisdom for Asia Bible College...to house forty-two "young Timothy's" during their three year training in Wisdom. Our Monthly Support helps them to run the Bible College and establish new churches in the villages of India. Our Partnership and generous Seeds are truly making a difference in the lives of the people in India!

We are going to see an unprecedented move of God in the coming months. India is home for over one billion people...thirty-three million gods and goddesses...their hunger for truth unmet...their thirst for Living Water unquenched...until Now.

Your Seeds into The Wisdom Center...are catalysts to Revival. Only Eternity will reveal the explosive power and energy of your Seeds, Prayers and Love-in-Action.

Your Mission Seed this month will truly make a difference.

Expecting An Uncommon Harvest,

*Mike*

WISDOM FOR ASIA BIBLE COLLEGE
PALELY, KATTAKADA, TVPM. 72.

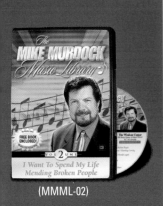

(MMML-02)

Ask for your Personal Gift Music CD, *I Want To Spend My Life Mending Broken People*, Volume 2, of the Mike Murdock Music Library... powerful songs ushering in the Presence of God all around the world.

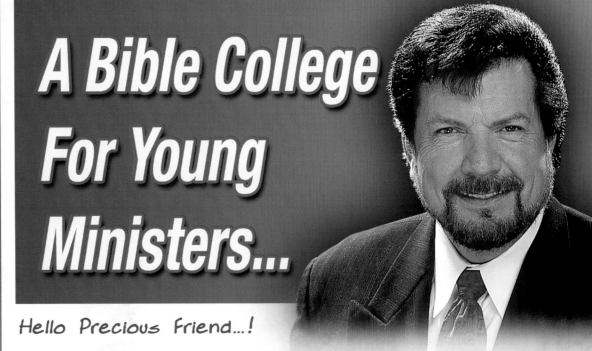

# A Bible College For Young Ministers...

Hello Precious Friend...!

For over 20 years, I have provided scholarships for young men and women of God, to train for the ministry. The possibilities of a Miracle Harvest on such a Significant Seed into the lives of "Young Timothy's"...are staggering. I have built my life around the Voice of The Holy Spirit. I was so sure you would want to know about this Uncommon Opportunity to shake India with young revivalists... "Young Timothys." **Wisdom is the answer to any human dilemma.** Even a small light shines brightly...in thick spiritual darkness. Together with your Special Mission Seed for training young ministers, we can ignite the fires of Wisdom throughout Asia... and around the world.

"Pray ye that the Lord of the Harvest, raise up Laborers..." (See Luke 10:2)

Expecting An Uncommon Harvest,

*Mike*

PS. Your Seed is helping to train young ministers and preach the gospel around the world. Remember to request your personal copy of my Gift Music CD, *"I Want To Spend My Life Mending Broken People"*.

The Wisdom Center • 4051 Denton Highway • Fort Worth, TX • Ph: (817) 759-0300 • www.TheWisdomCenter.tv

---

# Yes, Mike, I Want To Help Train Young Ministers In India And Around The World.

PLEASE REMOVE THIS PORTION AND RETURN IT IN THE ENCLOSED ENVELOPE.

NBYM1 ☐ Enclosed is My **Special Seed of $**_____ to help train young ministers in India and around the world.

NBYM2 ☐ Enclosed is My **Wisdom Key 3000** Monthly Faith Promise of $58 to help you spread the Gospel.

BYMGA ☐ Please Rush My Gift Music CD...*I Want To Spend My Life Mending Broken People.*
(This is Volume 2 of the new Collector's Edition of The Mike Murdock Music Library!) (MMML-02)

(MMML-02)

NAME _____

ADDRESS _____

CITY _____ STATE _____ ZIP CODE _____

PHONE _____ E-MAIL _____

**Method of Payment** *(Your check may be electronically deposited.)*
☐ MONEY ORDER ☐ CHECK ☐ AMEX
☐ DISCOVER ☐ MASTER CARD ☐ VISA

CARD #_____-_____-_____-_____

EXP. DATE ____/____ TOTAL ENCLOSED $_____

SIGNATURE _____
(SORRY NO C.O.D.'s)

63

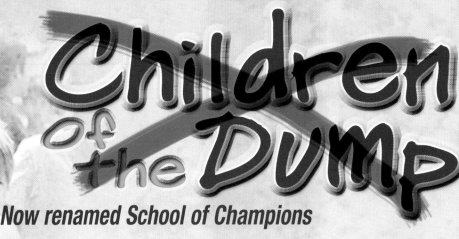

# Children of the Dump

## Now renamed School of Champions

Children matter.

A child is a Gift from God.

Imagine your child…without shoes…without clothing. Imagine your child without your embrace and affirmation…without anyone to demonstrate to them the Love of God.

Children observe. They absorb. They are like "containers." In their ears we deposit faith or fear, victory or defeat, motivation or depression. Unfortunately, in their early years they are unable to push the "reject" button when error is introduced. We want them to feel the Love of God…through our provision…!

You as a Faithful Partner, currently help feed 1,000 children in Mexico every day. Children of the Dump… renamed School of Champions brings relief and hope to the needy children and families living *in* and *around* the dump communities of Puerto Vallarta, Mexico. This wonderful organization is under the effective supervision of Bishop Saúl González-Vargas.

Together we can make a difference touching the world… one child at a time.

Your Love-Seed for our children is so appreciated!

*Your Love Seed of $31 a month…will feed a child who has been abandoned at The Dump… left to search for food and security without the love of a parent. "Inasmuch as ye have done it unto one of the least of these…ye have done it unto me," (Matthew 25:40).*

Children…are counting on you.

*Mike*

Bishop Saul Gonzalez-Vargas

(MMML-01)

Ask for your personal Gift Music CD, *The Sun Will Shine Again*, Volume 1, of the Mike Murdock Music Library... powerful songs ushering in the Presence of God all around the world.

# The School of Champions

Precious Partner,

Your Precious Seed will stop hopelessness and pain for hurting children. Hunger...especially for a child...is the loudest voice he hears. I really believe that children can experience the love of Jesus Christ. Together we are making a difference. What You Make Happen For Others, God Will Make Happen For You.

*Mike*

PS. When you sow your Special Seed of $31 or more, remember to request your personal Gift Music CD, *The Sun Will Shine Again!* Your Reaction To A Child Determines God's Reaction To You. *(Matthew 18:6)*

The Wisdom Center • 4051 Denton Highway • Fort Worth, TX • Ph: (817) 759-0300 • www.TheWisdomCenter.tv

- - - - - - - - - - - - - - - - - - - - - - - - - - - - - - - - - - - - - - - - - - - - - - - - - - - - - - - -

## Yes, Mike, I Want To Make A Difference In Mexico And Around The World...!

PLEASE REMOVE THIS PORTION AND RETURN IT IN THE ENCLOSED ENVELOPE.

(MMML-01)

NBFC1 ☐ Enclosed is My **Special Seed of $31** to help feed children and minister the gospel around the world.

NBFC2 ☐ Enclosed is My **Wisdom Key 3000** Monthly Faith Promise of $58 to help you spread the Gospel.

BFCGA ☐ Please Rush My Gift Music CD...***The Sun Will Shine Again!***
(This is Volume 1 of the new Collector's Edition of The Mike Murdock Music Library!) (MMML-01)

NAME

ADDRESS

CITY      STATE      ZIP CODE

PHONE      E-MAIL

**Method of Payment** *(Your check may be electronically deposited.)*
☐ MONEY ORDER  ☐ CHECK  ☐ AMEX
☐ DISCOVER  ☐ MASTER CARD  ☐ VISA

CARD #_____-_____-_____-_____

EXP. DATE ____/____   TOTAL ENCLOSED $_____

SIGNATURE _____
(SORRY NO C.O.D.'s)

65

# CHAMPIONS 4
## Book Pak!

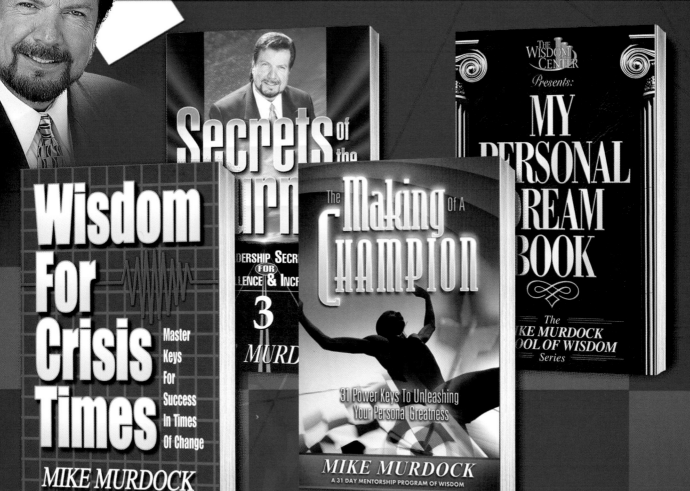

1. **Secrets of The Journey, Vol. 3** /<u>Book</u> (32pg/B-94/$5)

2. **My Personal Dream Book**/<u>Book</u> (32pg/B-143/$5)

3. **Wisdom For Crisis Times**/<u>Book</u> (112pg/B-40/$9)

4. **The Making Of A Champion** /<u>Book</u> (128pg/B-59/$10)

The Wisdom Center
Champions 4
Book Pak!
Only $20 $29 Value
PAK-23
Wisdom Is The Principal Thing

*This offer expires December 31st, 2007.    **Each Wisdom Book may be purchased separately if so desired.

Add 10% For S/H

# *Increase 4* *Book Pak!*

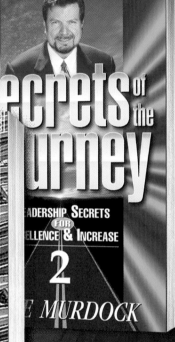

1. **Seeds of Wisdom on The Word of God**/<u>Book</u> (32pg/B-117/$5)
2. **Secrets of The Journey, Vol. 2**/<u>Book</u> (32pg/B-93/$5)
3. **7 Keys to 1000 Times More**
   /<u>Book</u> (128pg/B-104/$10)
4. **31 Secrets for Career Success**
   /<u>Book</u> (114pg/B-44/$10)

The Wisdom Center
**Increase 4 Book Pak!**
Only **$20** $30 Value
PAK-26
Wisdom Is The Principal Thing

**THE WISDOM CENTER**
4051 Denton Highway • Fort Worth, TX 76117

**1-888-WISDOM-1**
**1-817-759-0300**

Website:
TheWisdomCenter.tv

# Unforgettable Woman 4
## Book Pak!

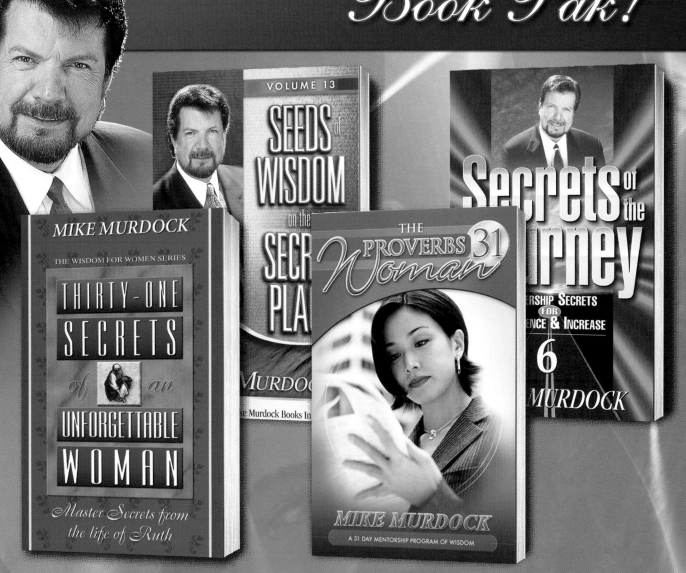

**1** Seeds of Wisdom on The Secret Place/<u>Book</u> (32pg/B-115/$5)

**2** Secrets of The Journey, Vol. 6/<u>Book</u> (32pg/B-102/$5)

**3** Thirty-One Secrets of an Unforgettable Woman/<u>Book</u> (140pg/B-57/$9)

**4** The Proverbs 31 Woman/<u>Book</u> (70pg/B-49/$7)

The Wisdom Center
**Unforgettable Woman 4 Book Pak!**
Only $**20**$26 Value
PAK-31
Wisdom Is The Principal Thing

*This offer expires December 31st, 2007.   **Each Wisdom Book may be purchased separately if so desired.

Add 10% For S/H

**THE WISDOM CENTER**
4051 Denton Highway • Fort Worth, TX 76117

**1-888-WISDOM-1**
**1-817-759-0300**

Website:
TheWisdomCenter.tv

*69*

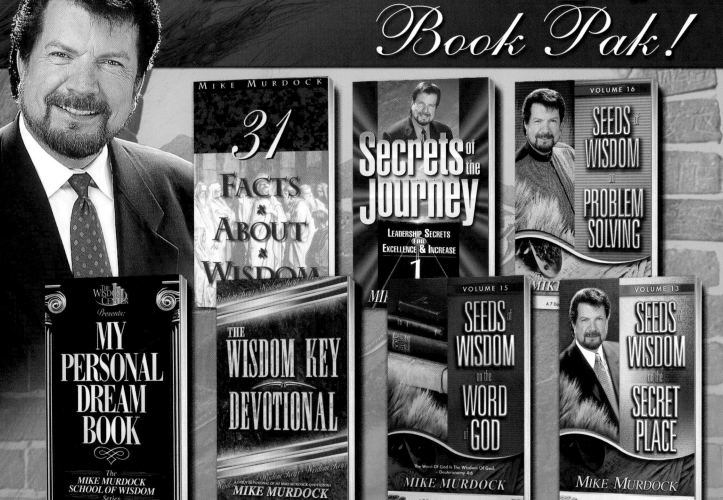

# The Mentorship 7 Book Pak!

**1 31 Facts About Wisdom**
/Book (32pg/B-46/$5)

**2 Secrets of The Journey, Vol. 1**
/Book (32pg/B-92/$5)

**3 Seeds of Wisdom on Problem-Solving** /Book (32pg/B-118/$5)

**4 My Personal Dream Book**
/Book (32pg/B-143/$5)

**5 The Wisdom Key Devotional**
/Book (60pg/B-165/$8)

**6 Seeds of Wisdom on The Word of God** /Book (32pg/B-117/$5)

**7 Seeds of Wisdom on The Secret Place** /Book (32pg/B-115/$5)

## All 7 Books For One Great Price!

The Wisdom Center
**The Mentorship 7 Book Pak!**
Only $20 $38 Value
PAK-25
Wisdom Is The Principal Thing

Add 10% For S/H

THE WISDOM CENTER
4051 Denton Highway • Fort Worth, TX 76117
**1-888-WISDOM-1**
**1-817-759-0300**
Website:
TheWisdomCenter.tv

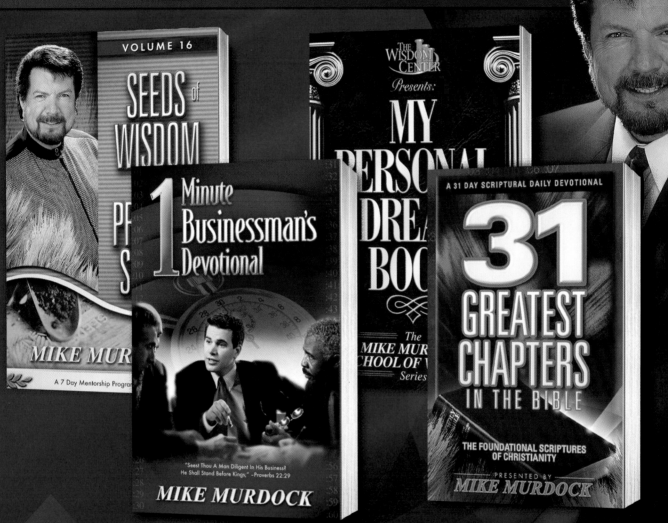

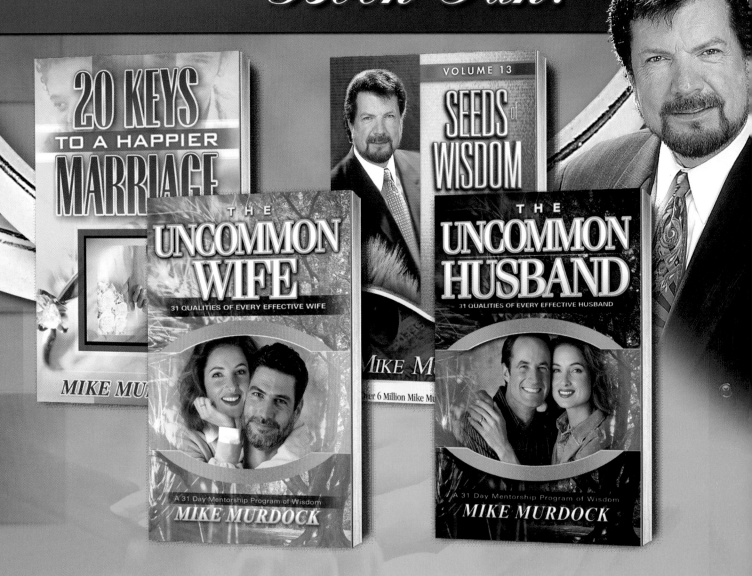

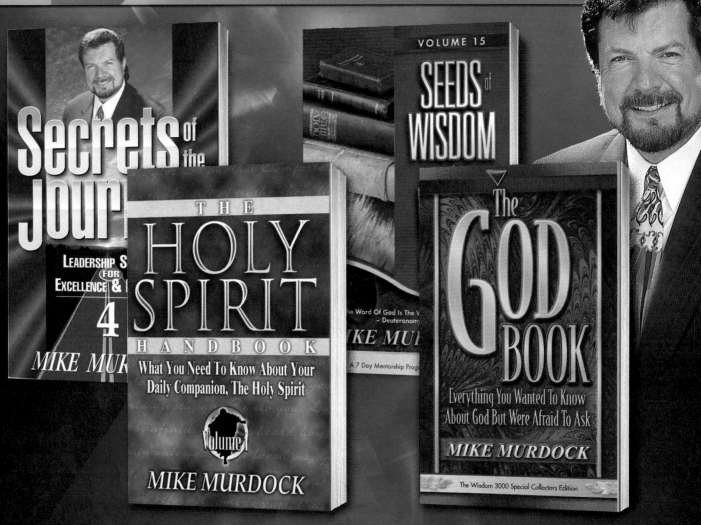

# GOD SECRETS 4 *Book Pak!*

**1** **Secrets of The Journey, Vol. 4**/<u>Book</u> (32pg/B-95/$5)

**2** **Seeds of Wisdom on The Word of God** /<u>Book</u> (32pg/B-117/$5)

**3** **The Holy Spirit Handbook**/<u>Book</u> (153pg/B-100/$10)

**4** **The God Book**/<u>Book</u> (160pg/B-26/$10)

The Wisdom Center
**God Secrets 4 Book Pak!**
Only $**20** $30 Value
PAK-27
*Wisdom Is The Principal Thing*

*This offer expires December 31st, 2007. **Each Wisdom Book may be purchased separately if so desired.

Add 10% For S/H

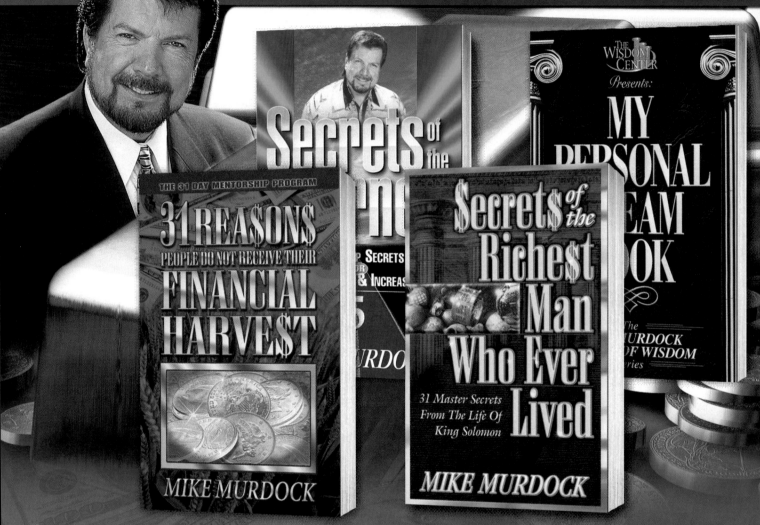

# Prosperity Secrets 4
## Book Pak!

**1** **Secrets of The Journey, Vol. 5** /Book (32pg/B-96/$5)

**2** **My Personal Dream Book**/Book (32pg/B-143/$5)

**3** **31 Reasons People Do Not Receive Their Financial Harvest**/Book (252pg/B-82/$12)

**4** **Secrets of the Richest Man Who Ever Lived** /Book (179pg/B-99/$10)

The Wisdom Center
**Prosperity Secrets 4 Book Pak!**
Only **$20** $32 Value
PAK-28
Wisdom Is The Principal Thing

THE WISDOM CENTER
4051 Denton Highway • Fort Worth, TX 76117

**1-888-WISDOM-1**
**1-817-759-0300**

Website:
TheWisdomCenter.tv

# The Double Diamond Devotional 4 Book Pak!

VOLUME 15

SEEDS of WISDOM on the WORD of GOD

The Wisdom Of God. Deuteronomy 4:6

MURDOCK

Program of Wisdom

MIKE MURDOCK

31 FACTS ABOUT WISDOM

THE Double Diamond PRINCIPLE

58 SUCCESS SECRETS IN THE LIFE OF JESUS

MIKE MURDOCK

THE Double Diamond Daily Devotional

365 Daily Inspirations For Extraordinary Achievers & Leaders

MIKE MURDOCK

**1** Seeds of Wisdom on The Word of God/<u>Book</u> (32pg/B-117/$5)

**2** 31 Facts About Wisdom /<u>Book</u> (32pg/B-46/$5)

**3** The Double Diamond Principle
   /<u>Book</u> (148pg/B-39/$9)

**4** The Double Diamond Daily Devotional
   /<u>Book</u> (378pg/B-72/$15)

The Wisdom Center
The Double Diamond Devotional 4 Book Pak!
Only $20 $34 Value
PAK-29
Wisdom Is The Principal Thing

DISCOVER

MasterCard

VISA

Add 10% For S/H

*This offer expires December 31st, 2007. **Each Wisdom Book may be purchased separately if so desired.

THE WISDOM CENTER
4051 Denton Highway • Fort Worth, TX 76117

1-888-WISDOM-1
1-817-759-0300

Website:
TheWisdomCenter.tv

75

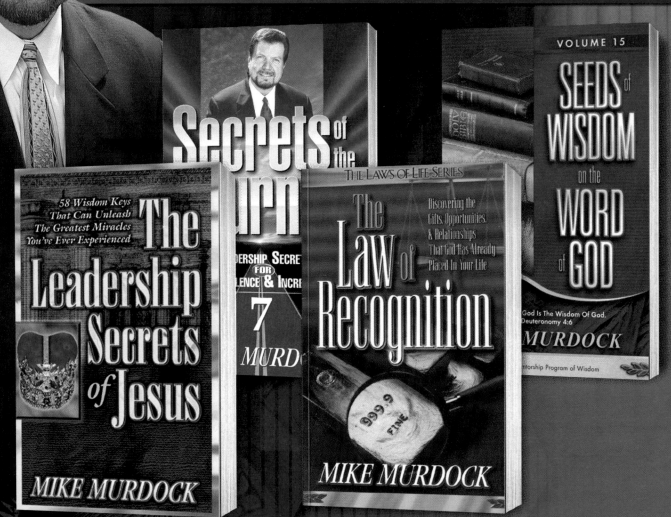

# The Laws of Leadership 4 Book Pak!

1 **Secrets of The Journey, Vol. 7**/Book (32pg/B-103/$5)

2 **Seeds of Wisdom on The Word of God** /Book (32pg/B-117/$5)

3 **The Leadership Secrets of Jesus**
/Book (196pg/B-91/$10)

4 **The Law of Recognition**
/Book (247pg/B-114/$10)

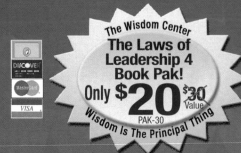

The Wisdom Center
**The Laws of Leadership 4 Book Pak!**
Only $20 $30 Value
PAK-30
Wisdom Is The Principal Thing

Add 10% For S/H

THE WISDOM CENTER
4051 Denton Highway • Fort Worth, TX 76117

1-888-WISDOM-1
1-817-759-0300

Website:
TheWisdomCenter.tv

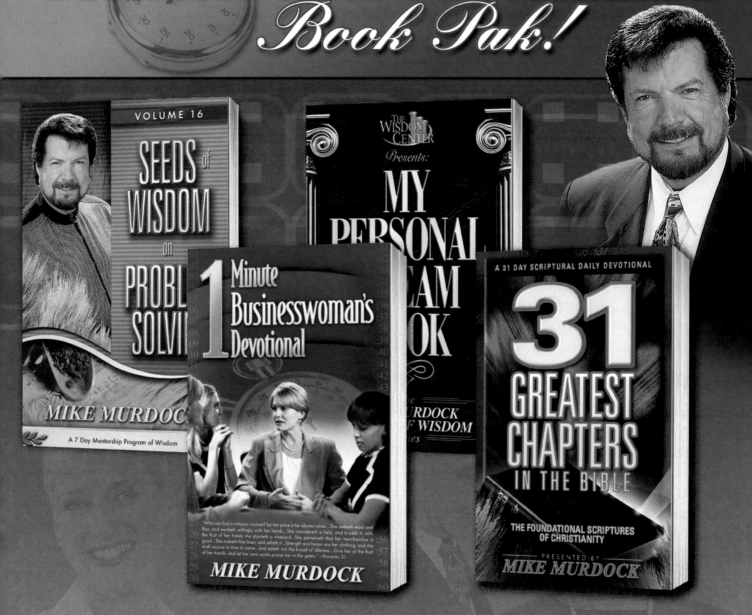

# The Millionaire 300

## THE UNCOMMON MILLIONAIRE $UCCE$$ SYSTEM (Series 1-3) [CD]

Money is a tool to produce and create good things for other people.

Throughout the Scriptures, God has always promised Uncommon Financial Provision for those who are obedient to His laws and statutes (Deuteronomy 28:1-14/Psalm 112:1-3).

Years ago, an anointing swept over me while I was in prayer in The Secret Place here in my home where have lived for the past 25 years. While praying, I envisioned 300 Christian Business People kneeling in the presence of God. They were seeking a divine Mantle of Prosperity and Favor to come upon their life. Their heart's goal was for anointed hands for Uncommon Productivity that would unleash *financial* blessing. I asked The Holy Spirit to pour divine Wisdom through my mind, my mouth and my ministry...and raise up **300 Problem-Solvers** who would become Millionaires for the Cause of Christ. I call them Uncommon Millionaires...because they would give God the glory, the praise and all the honor and stay humble and obedient to the mentorship voice of The Holy Spirit.

Pray about joining **The Millionaire 300...**and sowing a special Seed of $300 into this work and vision.

My special Gift to celebrate your membership and Seed is The Uncommon Millionaire Success System.

*Mike*

**Are You Drowning In A Sea Of Debt?** Receive an unforgettable impartation of Secrets of Financial Mentorship from proven Financial Achievers and Uncommon Millionaires who have studied the Laws of Blessing.

**Do You Dream Of Being An Uncommon Millionaire?** The steps to becoming a Millionaire will surprise you...it is not what you think! Be ready to receive the rewards of your faith.

**Accurately Applied These Truths Can Set You On The Path You Never Before Dreamed Possible.**

You Will Learn...
- Wise Investment Techniques Used By Uncommon Millionaires
- The Three Steps To A Debt-Free Lifestyle
- What To Do When You Face A Tax Or Credit Crisis
- What To Do When You Have Made A Major Financial Mistake
- Five Keys To Making Financial Decisions
- How To Get Out Of Debt And Become An Uncommon Financial Champion For The Kingdom Of God
- Tips On Estate Planning
- How To Rebuild Your Credit When You Have Made Great Mistakes
- The Hidden Secrets To Managing Your Time Effectively
- What To Do When You Have Made A Major Financial Mistake
- Five Keys To Effective Negotiation

*18 LIVE Mentorship Sessions!*

*Cannot Be Purchased*

MY GIFT OF APPRECIATION
*My Celebration Seed for those who join The Millionaire 300 and sow a Special Seed of $300 for the Work of God.*
CDPAK-01
Wisdom Is The Principal Thing

The Wisdom Center • 4051 Denton Highway • Fort Worth, TX 76117